Waiora

Waiora

Te Ūkaipō - The Homeland

A play by
HONE KOUKA

With waiata composed by
HONE HURIHANGANUI

HUIA PUBLISHERS

First Published in 1997 by Huia Publishers,
39 Pipitea Street, P O Box 17-335,
Wellington, Aotearoa New Zealand.

ISBN 0-908975-27-9

Text © Hone Kouka
Waiata © Hone Hurihanganui
This edition © Huia Publishers

Cover photos by Justine Lord
Cover design by Mark Geard
Designed, typeset and printed in Aotearoa New Zealand.

All applications to:
Playmarket
PO Box 9767
Wellington, New Zealand
ph 64-4-382 8462

Published with the support of Creative New Zealand Toi Aotearoa.

Kia tau te rangimārie
ki a tātou katoa.

For Maarire
So that she will know something of her Papa

Acknowledgements

Thanks to the New Zealand International Festival of the Arts for commissioning the piece, Creative New Zealand for financial support and Bell Gully Weir (Wellington), our generous sponsor of the original production.

A special thanks to all involved with the original production. The music, set and lighting design, direction and performance created a lasting impression.

To our kaumātua, Bob Wiki, for giving guidance and support.

Finally, thanks to Playmarket, Murray, Hone, Phillipa Campbell and the whānau of Downstage Theatre for their support.

Contents

Foreword

Māori are travellers. Sea people and land people, we are always on the move. Hone Kouka describes *Waiora* as "not just a Māori story but an immigrant's story. Something so many New Zealanders might be able to relate to – Scots, Chinese, German – all of us who have travelled from somewhere else". Yet for Māori that "somewhere else" in *Waiora* is the migration in their own homelands; the migration from rural, more traditional ways, to the city and an ever-fragmenting sense of self and past.

Indeed, *Waiora* places at its centre 18 year old Rongo, a Māori woman mourning the loss of many things: her nanny; the whānau and sense of place she had back in Waiora; te reo Māori; a family slipping further away from the raranga that joins land and sky.

Waiora, both as a text and as a piece of live theatre, shows much of what is best in Māori theatre. The writing shimmers softly but has a strong undercurrent that tugs long after the words have swum past. In performance *Waiora* initially seems light on the surface but it slowly draws an audience in with the tightly structured insistency of its voices.

Kouka has filtered both the experiences of his family and his own involvement in Māori and New Zealand theatre into *Waiora*. The play can be seen as a formal realisation of many components of contemporary Māori theatre.

Numerous Māori plays, from the 1970s through to the late 1990s, have included these themes or components: a strong sense of association with the past and tūpuna; loss; longing for what has gone or been taken; land as central to identity; the search for identity or a changing or shifting sense of identity or self; the discovery of family secrets – especially in relation to whakapapa or breaches of tapu; the arrival of a stranger as a portent of future happenings or things hidden in the past; the fight to survive intact as whānau and as a culture; conflict with authority – often in the form of government or Pākehā control; whānau or hapu/iwi rivalries; contested leadership; spiritual forces as omnipresent, influencing all times; the special position of whāngai; inclusion of cultural forms such as haka, karanga and wero; tangi; hope for the unity or integration of whānau or individuals.

Māori theatre is a theatre that constantly remembers the past. I cannot recall having seen a play by a Māori writer that did not make some reference to tūpuna. The emanations/spirits of the dead most certainly rattle our bones. It is our ancestors who remind us of who we are, where we belong, and why we have been given the gift of life. Tūpuna and ngā Atua Māori are all central to the way in which *Waiora* is structured. These Atua steer the play through the stormy passage of change. The whānau are beached, far away from the support of ther relations and the safety of their tūrangawaewae.

Rongo understands the need to accept the harsh but ultimately healing challenges that Papatūānuku and Tangaroa throw at her feet. She has the chance of aligning herself with the forces of nature and whakapapa so that a kind of healing – the reunification of the whānau – can take place. Death of mauri, of memory and of self is the alternative. A kind of genocidal amnesia is proffered by Pākehā society and to some degree accepted in the uneasy, ritualised relationships between the Māori family and the Pākehā mill owner and school teacher.

The wrath of Whiro stirs the emotions of a father lost (John/ Hone). His is a punishing facade, one that hides a man caught between cultures and roles, a man already re-enacting the negative 'traditions' of his own childhood. Ultimately, the spirituality he has suppressed is also his redemption.

Tangaroa asserts the power of the sea and tidal reaches, places of bounty and of danger. The characters in the play seem to float, to bob on water, as though trying to keep upright. The beach, with its abundance of kaimoana, is also a place of un- known consequences, a place where tides can capture as well as give.

Papatūānuku is always with us. She is the mother, the ūkaipō, the place of nourishment and energising acceptance that Rongo cries out for.

Ranginui fans the fire that almost leaps out of control. His breath moves amongst the whānau turning them in each direction to examine their own rigidity and relationships.

Tāne Mahuta could be seen as being aligned with the mill that both Māori and Pākehā characters work at. Mill owner's son Steve unwittingly says to John/Hone: "[s]ure there isn't sap in your veins?" – a many faceted line indeed. It brings to mind the remnant strength of Tāne as he is cut, dressed and sold to others, his 'blood' seeping into the hands of John/Hone who increasingly becomes a 'sap', drained by the political circumstances of the time. Tāne's sheltering embrace contin- ues to be felled as John/Hone seeks status from the mill man- ager.

While *Waiora* looks at Pākehā expectations of Māori from the safety that distance provides it does not seek to either challenge directly or to provide a comfortable avoidance of reality. Kouka touches on things that many New Zealanders prefer to forget. As one of Kouka's uncles remarked to him, "not much has changed for us really. Not much at all." Kouka frames Pākehā paternalism and non-acceptance of Māori from a Māori viewpoint.

At the beginning of the play the tīpuna call the family to come together to work as one; by the end the whānau have realised how important their traditions are. It is John/Hone, Rongo's father, who must finally speak in his own tongue, entreat his daughter to return to life, a life in which her whole being has longed for the return to Waiora, te ūkaipō, their homeland. Seeing the first production of *Waiora* was a homecoming in itself. Here was a production that kept intact many of the things that we can now say have become part of the whakapapa of Māori theatre development, practice and performance. *Waiora* is evidence of the craft that Hone has as a writer and the fine work and direction that Murray Lynch has imbued the production with.

Roma Potiki

First Performance

Waiora was first presented for the New Zealand International Festival of the Arts 1996 at Downstage Theatre, Wellington, on 15 March 1996, with the following cast and crew:

Hone (John)	Rawiri Paratene
Wai Te Atatu (Sue)	Tina Cook
Amiria	Rachael House
Rongo	Nancy Brunning
Boyboy	Jason Te Kare
Steve Campbell	Mick Rose
Louise Stones	Nicky Murphy
The Tīpuna	Antonio Te Maioha
	Grace Hoet
	Karl Kite Rangi
	Toni Huata
Kaumātua	Bob Wiki
Director	Murray Lynch
Script	Hone Kouka
Haka and Waiata	Hone Hurihanganui
Script Advisor	Phillipa Campbell
Musical Director	Laughton Patrick
Set Design & Costume	John Parker
Lighting Design	Ivan Morundi
Stage Management	Anthony Hodgkin
Producer	Fenn Gordon

Characters

The Whānau

HONE (JOHN)
Father of the whānau, in his late thirties, has worked outdoors all his life. Had been to the city perhaps once as a child,
so his perception is somewhat distorted. Moved to the city
for work and a better life for his family.

WAI TE ATATU (SUE)
Mother, wife and trusted friend. Same age as Hone. Will go
with her husband, wherever he goes. She too puts her family
before anything. Would work from sunrise to sunset for her
children. She had them in her teens. She has spent some time
in the city.

AMIRIA
Eldest daughter. 19. A beauty, she is not cut of the same cloth
as her brothers and sister. Wants the city life, finds the country constricting. Looks upon herself as Pākehā, not Māori.
Move to the city is a means of escape. Loves music.

BOYBOY
Pōtiki. 15-16. A loner, quiet. Like his father, yearns for the
outdoors. A hunter. Good sportsman.

RONGO
Daddy's girl.18.Tūturu Māori. Close to her tīpuna. Has lost
something since leaving Waiora. Sings like a tui.

The People

STEVE CAMPBELL
Hone's boss, Pākehā, in his late thirties, early forties. Took over as boss from his father in the family business. Sporty, but not a sportsman. Honest and true.

LOUISE STONES
Secondary school teacher. As a woman at a secondary school, is very different. She isn't a local either. In her twenties, liberal, brought up in the country, so connects with whānau through that. Outspoken.

THE TĪPUNA
This group of four people are all Māori. They are there primarily to give more texture to mass scenes and also act as a metaphor for what the whānau are leaving behind. This group in later scenes almost haunts the family. They should be dressed neutrally, close to the other characters. The main focus for them is Rongo; she is the reason they are at the hāngi.

THE STRANGER
One of the Tīpuna.

Setting

The east coast of the South Island. A beach. Late summer.

Prologue

*Early morning. An empty beach stretching far into the distance,
a blue wash covers it; flickers of light coming from the water.
Back from the sea and behind flecked sand dunes is a clearing,
bare and empty. Four figures appear in the waking light. They
are TĪPUNA. After surveying the place, they quietly begin to
sing the waiata 'Taukuri E'. It is slow and mournful, talking of
the pain of leaving the papa kāinga. They are preparing the place
for the events of the day.*

Taukuri e...   Aue rā, e te hau kāinga
                     Mākūkū ana i aku roimata

Taukuri e...   Te ūnga o te tāngaengae
                     E kukume noa nei te ate

Ranginui...   E tū nei titiro kau iho
                     ki ahau e whakarere atu nei

I a Papa...   Kia kāewaewa noa rā
                     kia tika ai ko te kimi oranga[1]

*Soon the whānau arrive. RONGO is first to enter. The whānau
then fall in behind her; the TĪPUNA welcome them to the place.
(The whānau are unable to see them.) They pull RONGO forward as she is the main focus for them this day. Lights and the
TĪPUNA should stay with her for some time. The whānau carry
with them what they need for the day: basins, baskets, some kai,
beer and crates to sit on. They look around, taking in the place,
and eventually set up for the day. Once the whānau is ready, the
lights should rise, like the glare of the city. As the TĪPUNA con-*

[1]See page 110 for English translation

tinue to sing 'Taukuri E', the whānau join in with a haka to the city they have recently come to.

Kaitataki   Ko te hūnuku e... iee
          Ko te hūnuku e... iee

Tauā   Ko te hūnuku tokoiti ki te pae tawhiti ki te whai
          oranga tinana tangata...

Kaitataki   Aue rā ko te rama!

Tauā   Kapakapa ake nei!

Kaitataki   Kī nei i te tangata!

Tauā   Kiritea nei hoki!
          Tukuna mai ōu painga, tukuna mai ōu whērū
          hoki.
          Kia rongohia te kino, te reka, te aha, te aha o
          te ao hurihuri nei nā e... ie!!
          Taukuri e... Aue rā...[2]

This section with the whānau and TĪPUNA is non-naturalistic and is stylised in the images it throws forward. The haka and the waiata from the two groups comes to a close. The TĪPUNA slowly make their way off, watching the whānau as they go, most especially HONE. From time to time through the play they will reappear, guiding the family, putting up barriers, tasks for the whānau to get through. The whānau move to where they begin the play proper; they all stop stock-still, take in a deep breath and then begin.

[2]See pages 110-111 for English translation

Act 1

Tīmata

The year is 1965. The setting is a small cove on the east coast of Te Waipounamu (the South Island). It is near the end of a long hot summer, March. The beach in the cove has a span of sand that touches the water. Smooth stones and rocks ride piggy-back across it. Behind that are banks lined with tussock, scrub and grass.

We see HONE. He is in his late thirties, a strongly built man, obviously used to working outdoors. He wears a singlet, moleskin trousers and boots. A butcher's knife and steel hang from his side; he is cutting up meat.

Moving around, never still, is WAI, Hone's wife. She is of the same age. Their daughters, AMIRIA and RONGO, are helping also. All women are well-dressed and aprons cover their clothing.

There is also a Pākehā woman with them. She seems very much at home. Her name is LOUISE STONES, a school teacher at the local high school. She is in her mid-twenties and dressed the same as the other women. She doesn't have an apron. All are rushing around preparing food; some sitting scrubbing vegetables, others cleaning. The purpose of this gathering is that it is RONGO's 18th birthday. AMIRIA and LOUISE begin to sing 'She Loves You' by the Beatles. The mood is light amongst everyone.

John/Hone   (*singing to himself, then calling back to AMIRIA and LOUISE*) Amelia Rose, what the hell do you call that racket?! (*laughs*)

Amiria   It's the Beatles Dad! *(she begins to sing again)*

John/Hone   Who? The Bugs! Sounds more like you're skinning a cat, if you ask me. *(he mimics the song)* Are they those Pommy fullas eh?! You know, the best thing that ever came from there was the boats going back. *(laughs, then realising LOUISE)* Oh, sorry Louise, I didn't mean to be rude eh, just having a bit of a laugh.

Louise   It's alright. *(to AMIRIA)* I think you're all so funny, full of jokes.

Amiria   Eh?

Louise   Always laughing. I wish my family was funny. We're all as dry as a dog's biscuit.

Amiria   Yeah, yeah we are funny. Ha ha ha.

John/Hone   *(to RONGO)* Hey Rongo. *(no response)* Rongo! Baby!

Rongo   Yeah Dad.

John/Hone   You like that stuff as well? Those cat noises?! *(laughs)*

Amiria   No use asking her Dad, she thinks she's a kuia. *(laughs)* Eh Aunty, you alright? *(laughs)*

Rongo   You shut up, no I don't. *(beat)* Kei te pai Pā, I kinda like it.

John/Hone	Well I don't. Why don't you kids sing some real stuff? *(he sings the waiata 'Taku Patu Auē'. The* TĪPUNA *join in. He dances and grabs* WAI *as she is coming through. It slowly fades)* You never sing them now. How come?
Amiria	Because you said we weren't allowed to.
John/Hone	*(to self)* Probably 'cause I said you weren't allowed to. Don't have the characters here to sing them anyhow... Uncle Taite, he was still singing the favourites when we went back for Christmas. What's that one he always sings?
Sue/Wai	*(passing)* 'He Putiputi!'
John/Hone	That's right, 'He putiputi pai katohia, he piri ki te uma e... i te... ' oh... what was it? What... oh bloody hell, I forgot it. We only been away for a while and I'm forgetting already.
Amiria	*(to self) 'and you know you should be glad...'*
John/Hone	Eh?!
Amiria	Just singing Dad.
Sue/Wai	You never knew the words to start with, that's why you forgot them. You silly fool. *(laughs)*
John/Hone	No, I did. I did.
Sue/Wai	No you didn't. If you're mokemoke for whānau, remember Missy's coming down soon.

John/Hone   Yeah, sounds like all the 'rellies' are, now we settled in. Soon we'll have all of Waiora here eh?! *(laughs)*

BOYBOY *enters carrying baskets for the food.*

Boyboy   Kei te pai tēnā.[3] *(beat)* Hello Miss Stones.

Louise   Hello Boy.

John/Hone   Eh... ? How's that fire going? You keeping an eye on it?! What the hell are you doing here anyway, eh?

Boyboy   You asked me to bring the basket over. *(to his father)* Kua reri ngā kai? Nā te mea kua wera. Kei te pai te ahi, nē Dad? E kore e taea e au te tatari ki te whakatakoto i te hāngi.[4]

John/Hone   What did I say?

Boyboy   Don't speak Māori here.

John/Hone   That's right, not here. Are you listening?

Boyboy   Yeah Dad, I heard you. Sorry Dad, sorry, I just forget sometimes. I forget. *(excited)* Kei te wareware ahau.

John/Hone   Well remember. It's for your own good, Boy.

Sue/Wai   Leave him, he made a mistake. Didn't you Boy? Just a mistake.

[3] 'Wouldn't be so bad'

[4] 'Is the food ready? 'Cause the fire's hotting up, I can't wait to put the hāngi down. It'll be good, eh Dad?'

John/Hone   He's always making mistakes. If Mahurangi was here...

Sue/Wai   But he isn't.

John/Hone   No.

Sue/Wai   (*to* HONE) Go and do your job and stop being a grumpy old sod.

John/Hone   I'll 'grumpy old sod' you in a minute.

RONGO *goes to exit.*

John/Hone   Oi! Where are you going, Baby?

Rongo   Down to the beach. I can stay if you got more for me to do.

Amiria   Yeah, 'cause there's more to do, you can't just take off. (*under her breath*) Daddy's Girl.

Rongo   What was that? Shut up, I pull my weight. If there's anyone who skives off, it's you, tiko bum!

Amiria   You're the one who stinks! And I don't take off all the time! If you don't shut up, I'll whack you.

Rongo   Go on then!

They fight.

John/Hone	Hey! Hey! Hey you two, like we almost got a war on our hands. Amiria, you leave her alone. You two always at each other, yep, yep, yep, yep, yep, just like your aunties, all the bloody time. *(beat)* So, where you going, baby?
Rongo	Ki te moana. I asked Mum – she said it was alright.
John/Hone	*(to* WAI*)* Did you let her?
Sue/Wai	Āe.
John/Hone	Well we can't argue with the boss then, can we, and since it's your birthday, 'way ya go.
Amiria	Oh Mum!
Sue/Wai	It's her birthday, girl – your time will come.

RONGO *exits.*

Boyboy	Dad? How come you cut the meat so small?
John/Hone	It's for the Pākehā. Go and check the stones, see if the fire is hot enough. Oh, and keep wetting down the sacks. Make sure they're real wet, eh, and the watercress as well. Wet! (BOYBOY *doesn't move*) Well, don't just bloody stand there. Do it.

BOYBOY *exits.*

John/Hone   Oi! (*to* WAI)

Sue/Wai   What?!

John/Hone   (*to* WAI) Am I not here?

Sue/Wai   Looks like you're there to me. (*laughs at her own joke*)

John/Hone   Cheeky. Well, why the hell don't those kids listen to a word I say then?

Sue/Wai   Cause you don't have a wooden spoon in your hand when you say it. (*giggles*) They do, don't be stupid.

John/Hone   No they don't, what have you done with those kids?!

Sue/Wai   E kī me, you did it too buster.

John/Hone   But they're a pack of bloody dreamers. I didn't bring them up to be dreamers.

Sue/Wai   You're the one who put the dreams into their heads.

John/Hone   Oh no. (*laughing*) My Mum was right – don't marry into that whānau – always away with the fairies.

Sue/Wai   Eh, shut up you...

24

AMIRIA *and* LOUISE *start singing 'The Blue Beat'.*

John/Hone   That Louise, she doesn't act like a school teacher.

Sue/Wai   She's not much older than Amiria remember.

John/Hone   Still, a bloody school teacher. Should set an example or something.

Sue/Wai   Like you. *(laughs)* Let her have a good time, she's got her whole life to act like a grown up.

John/Hone   Oh, but... I just can't work her out, eh.

Sue/Wai   What are you getting at?

John/Hone   Well, you know.

Sue/Wai   No I don't. I can do most things but I can't read minds. Hey, you been at the booze already? I told you to wait till Mr Campbell got here...

John/Hone   Can't work out why she picked us.

Sue/Wai   Maybe 'cause she has no whānau here, I don't know. She's become my friend. I trust her, that's all that counts. *(beat)* The guest of honour will be arriving soon and we haven't even started to clean up. *(to* AMIRIA*)* Get a move on with those spuds. *(to* HONE*)* Shake a leg!

He shakes his leg comically.

Sue/Wai   Oh bloody pōrangi. You're worse than those kids sometimes. Come on Mr Foreman.

John/Hone   What did you say? Foreman?

Sue/Wai   Koretake more like it.

John/Hone   No, no Mr Foreman. Mr Foreman sounds like I been called it for years. *(beat)* It's all starting to work out – the move down, promotion on the way, everything. *(he gives her a peck on the cheek)* I'll go and get the extra stuff from the car.

He exits. WAI *goes over to* LOUISE *and* AMIRIA. *She is humming a tune.*

Louise   Sue, you look tickled pink.

Sue/Wai   I am, this, this is a... a...

Amiria   ...it's a good day, eh Mum?

Sue/Wai   That's the words, girl, – a good day. Now, let's get a move on eh? Everything's gotta be right, proper.

She moves away from the other two, cleaning and preparing.

Louise   Oh, Amelia...

26

Amiria   (*sarcastically*) Oh Louise... What?

Louise   Your Mum...

Amiria   Yeah, what about her?

Louise   She's like a young girl, she looks so happy. She was so excited about today. It's all she talked about the last time we saw each other.

Amiria   We don't talk. We work. (*pause*) Oh where did you get that dress from? Shouldn't be peeling spuds in that – it's too flash.

Louise   Oh, it's nothing really, quite old.

Amiria   Is it?

Louise   I was thinking of throwing it in the rag bag.

Amiria   Rags. (*laughs. She holds up a tea towel or the apron*) I'd love to have enough money to buy dress after dress, like that, dress after dress, 'Oh no, not that one. I'll have that one. No, that one. Yes thank you.' (*they both laugh*)

AMIRIA *and* LOUISE *tone down the laughter. They move into a slow motion, at times breaking out with laughter.* WAI *looks over at them.*

Sue/Wai   Laugh girl, she's got such a beautiful laugh. (*beat*) When she was a baby, she was happy with what she had. Not now, though. She'll be leaving us soon. She wants more.

Pause.

Louise Oh, Rongo's present, I left it in my car. Never mind, I'll get it later.

Sue/Wai You shouldn't have bothered about a present, Lou.

Louise It's not much.

Amiria *(sarcastically)* Rags?

Sue/Wai Don't be so cheeky, miss.

Louise She's OK. It isn't much – some lace handkerchiefs. *(beat)* Did you make Rongo that dress you were talking about?

Sue/Wai No, I um...

Amiria She couldn't afford the material.

Louise You should have said something. I've got yards of the stuff lying around at home.

Sue/Wai That's not why. John and I decided to give her a present we were saving till she got married.

Amiria Her get married? *(laughs)* Yeah, like I wanna go back to the Coast.

Sue/Wai Listen here, you!

Louise	She's just having you on, Sue.
Amiria	Yeah, just having you on.
Louise	So, what are you giving her instead?
Sue/Wai	A comb.
Louise	Oh that's nice.
Sue/Wai	It was her Nanny's.
Louise	Oh, a family heirloom. We have a silver cup that's been handed down. Three, four generations.
Sue/Wai	It's an old whalebone comb that her Nanny treasured. Rongo loved her Nanny so much...
Amiria	...was always with her.
Sue/Wai	The comb is to keep her safe.
Louise	Safe?
Sue/Wai	Mmm, safe.

Lights fade on them and they freeze. They come up on RONGO *on another part of the stage.* RONGO *is down at the beach. The* TĪPUNA *are with her. Water laps around her feet and in her hand a shell, a stone, something to remind her of the old woman, her grandmother. She is silent, but her mouth is moving. Slowly, the waiata she is singing fades up and we hear it. The waiata is 'Tawhiti'. The* TĪPUNA *have quietly raised their voices with her.*

Tawhiti, kei Hawaiiki pāmamao,
Kei Rangiātea nui...
Auē, tawhiti e

Āhuru, ko te whenua waiwaiā,
Te Moana-nui-a-Kiwa...
Auē, tawhiti e

Tukurere nei ko te wairua ki te kura-i-Awarua
ki ngā pārekereke kōrero
i ruia ake rā i Rangiātea

Mokemoke kau ana te ngākau i te hiringa
tawhito
i te mātāpuna haumanu
i te pū o taku whatumanawa

Kia kake rā te Aka Matua
I kake ai Tāwhaki
Kauā rā e ō ringaringa
E pā atu ki te Aka Taepa

Taku nui e, taku tiketike,
I ahu mai i aku tīpuna
Ēhara taku toa i te toa takitahi
Engari, he toa takimano...

Tawhiti... tawhiti.[5]

She finishes the waiata and begins to speak. The TĪPUNA gather around her.

---

[5] See pages 111-112 for English translation.

Rongo   Did you like that Nanny? It is one of the wai that you taught me. Kei te mahara ahau ki ngā pao, ngā waiata, ngā haka arā te katoa. E hika! kei te makariri te wai.[6] *(beat)* I am standing in the water so I can touch home. Kei te whānui ngā ringaringa o Tangaroa hei awhi a Papatūānuku.[7] His hands smooth out the sand you see. Pari mai, pari atu.[8] So if I am held in those hands, I am taken back to the beach of Waiora, our true home. Waiora Te Ūkaipō, The Homeland. *(beat)* Nanny, I'm so hungry, not for kai, but for words. Here, we kōrero Pākehā, not Māori. Not allowed to. E Nanny, kei te mataku ahau.[9] Scared I'll waste away to a whisper, then nothing, and I will forget our words, and if I do, my children will have nothing to eat. Their mouths will not know the taste we once knew, they will forget. But we are hurting ourselves. We are stopping ourselves from speaking the reo. No one is doing it to us. Dad said if we live like Pākehā, then they will leave us in peace and we will be strong. *(beat)* But what will we be? I don't think we will ever learn their ways. We will be a lost people first. We will. *(pause)* Auē e Nanny, whakarongo mai ki ahau, kei te whakarongo mai koe? Auē taukuri e. Tukua ahau kia haere i tō taha. *(beat)* I ngā wā katoa kei roto i a koe te kaha pūmau. E kui kei te pīrangi ahau i tō kaha, kī mai ki ahau. Kei te whakarongo mai koe, whakarongo mai![10] Lost.

---

[6] 'I remember the pao, waiata, haka, everything. Oh! The water is cold.'
[7] 'The hands of Tangaroa reach out along Papatūānuku.'
[8] 'Wash in, wash out.'
[9] 'I'm scared Nanny.'
[10] 'Oh Nanny, listen to me. Are you listening? Alas, take me with you. You were always so strong. I need your strength, speak to me. Are you listening? Listen!'

RONGO *bends down and scoops up a handful of water and slowly lets it trickle over her face. She is dejected.*

Ka ngaro.[11]

There is a silence. RONGO *turns to go. Meanwhile, the* TĪPUNA *have formed a line, in front or around her. They begin to haka. Immediately she sees them, at once frightened, and at the same time joyous.*

> Tēnei noa te whakahei atu nei
> Kia whakarauirihia aku pangore e kō...
>
> Kuhuna mai rā, kuhuna mai rā
> Ko Te korokoro-ā-te-Parata e kō...
>
> Tēnei rā ko te aumihi tīramarama ake nei
> He wheturangi – kanapa...
>
> Ko te ihi, ko te wehi, ko te wanawana
> E tō haere ake rā i a koe...
>
> Haere mai rā, haere mai rā, haere mai rā...
> e... i[12]

RONGO *is enjoying it now, the power of the haka pulling her in. Then, just as quickly, it ends and they disappear. The* TĪPUNA *remain on stage.* RONGO *is unable to see them. She is distraught.*

Rongo   Kaua e haere! Auē kei te ngaro koe, kei whea![13] (*beat*) If I go with you it will bring the family close together, you know that. Haria ahau i tō taha me koe e kui, haria ahau i tō taha![14]

---

[11] 'Lost.'
[12] See page 112 for English translation.
[13] 'Don't go! Where have you gone?!'
[14] 'Take me with you Nanny, take me with you!'

32

When no one returns, RONGO runs off. The TĪPUNA stay on stage. Lights fade and come up on the others back at the hāngi. The women are still preparing the food and tidying up. AMIRIA and LOUISE freeze. A shaft of light highlights WAI. She takes a sharp intake of breath. She seems startled.

Sue/Wai   Rongo! Kei whea a Rongo?!

The lights snap off her. AMIRIA and LOUISE begin to move. The TĪPUNA exit.

Amiria   Mum, you let her go down to the beach, remember. Jeez!

Sue/Wai   It's alright, she's alright.

Amiria   Mum, you saw something didn't you? Shall I go look for her?

Sue/Wai   I said, she's fine.

Louise   What was that? What... ?

Sue/Wai   Nothing to worry about, Lou.

Louise   Oh, well if you say so... mmm. (*to* WAI) Thank you for inviting me.

Sue/Wai   It's the least we could do – you been looking after our Boy.

Amiria   Yeah, we always forget about him, so it's good to have someone else looking out for him.

'Oh Boy, I forgot about you', 'Boy, what are you doing there?' The forgotten one. *(laughs)* Not like me, eh Mum? Can't forget me, cha cha cha!

Sue/Wai   True girl, can't forget you.

Pause.

Amiria   You like teaching Lou?

Louise   I suppose so.

Amiria   Suppose so?! Hey, why're you at a high school anyway? You after someone?

Sue/Wai   Hey! What have I said to you?!

Louise   It was a challenge. I don't know really why.

Amiria   Doesn't matter, I was only being nosy. I hate my job.

Sue/Wai   What?!

Amiria   I said, I hate my job. Don't worry, I'm not gonna leave. Not right now anyway.

Sue/Wai   Don't you go leaving it. Your father used a favour to get it for you.

Amiria   I said I'm not gonna leave. I just don't wanna spend my life working at a mill day in, day out. I got better things. I got dreams Mum, I got dreams.

Sue/Wai	We all got dreams girl, that's what got us here. *(beat)* Dad asked Mr Campbell to give you that job, so I want you to be thankful to him when he turns up.
Amiria	I will Mum, don't worry. I will.
Louise	Sue, there's something I wanted to talk to you about.
Sue/Wai	Fire away Lou, what is it?
Louise	It's about Boy...
Sue/Wai	Yes, what's he done now? *(chuckles)*
Louise	Well you see, he...

RONGO *comes running in. She is shivering.* WAI *goes to her.*

Sue/Wai	Baby where have you been?
Amiria	Mum, she's not a baby anymore.
Sue/Wai	Oh god girl, you're freezing. Were you stupid and go for a swim?!
Rongo	*(shivering)* No Mum.
Sue/Wai	But you're so cold.
Rongo	I was standing in the water.

Sue/Wai   That is a stupid thing to do. *(she is rubbing* RONGO's *feet)* This place is so cold. If we were back home...

Amiria   Mum!

Sue/Wai   But we're not.

BOYBOY *comes in.* WAI *leaves* RONGO.

Boyboy   Dad wants to know how much longer you're gonna be with the vegetables. The fire's getting lower. We'll be ready to put down the hāngi soon. *(excited)* He's gonna let me put it down. Me. My first hāngi. Che!

Sue/Wai   Oh, that's great son. Not too long Boy, tell him not too long. Sorry Lou, you wanted to talk to me about Boy.

Louise   *(she looks to* BOYBOY*)* Oh, it was nothing really. With all the excitement, I've forgotten.

Sue/Wai   Oh never mind, it'll come up later eh, I'm sure.

Louise   Yes it will.

Amiria   Jeez, you get excited pretty easy. Your boyfriend must be a lucky fella. Not been away from home much, eh white girl?! *(laughs)* We Māori too crazy! Cold feet from the sea, whoa pretty exciting! *(laughs)*

Sue/Wai   Stop getting cheeky, leave Lou alone. Boy, you'd better head back. Your Dad will be wild, you hanging around the women. Tell him soon eh?

BOYBOY *exits. The others go back to the vegetables.*

Louise   *(searching)* I'd love to, ah, 'put down' a hāngi myself. That's digging the hole and everything isn't it?

Sue/Wai   A lot more than that, Lou.

Louise   Is this how it always is?

Sue/Wai   What do you mean, Lou?

Amiria   Now, right me if I'm wrong, but I think she means do the wāhine always do this stuff, the vegetables and all that, and the tāne do the rest?

Louise   Yes, that's right. It looks like John and Boy are having a hoot doing that. I mean do we really have to do this? What fun they must be having!

Amiria   Oh yeah, what fun.

Sue/Wai   Who else would do it? You wanna cut down all the wood, find the right stones? We were the cooks in the past, but things change. The main thing is that we don't forget how to do it. Eh?

Amiria	Look Lou, if it was up to me we'd have no hāngis – why dig a hole in the ground and put a fire on top when you can use an oven? Bloody Maoris – when will we ever learn?
Louise	I don't know, I quite like it. Outside and all that. You people are lucky.
Rongo	You people?
Amiria	Oh, she lives. Here, you can finish those off. (*she hands* RONGO *some vegetables*)
Rongo	Mum?
Sue/Wai	What did you see?

The TĪPUNA *appear on stage. Quietly, the haka 'Tēnei noa te whakahei atu nei' is said underneath. Soon, it is only the actions, the* TĪPUNA *mouthing the words.* RONGO *is looking at them.*

Rongo	See? Oh, nothing.
Amiria	Yes you did, you know Mum's never wrong with things like this.
Louise	What things?
Amiria	Mum... whaddaya call it Mum? Mum ahh... sees things, feels things. Magic, scary huh?!
Sue/Wai	Amiria! (*to* RONGO) What did you see, Baby?

The TĪPUNA *end the haka and exit.*

Rongo   Nothing... it was nothing eh... I didn't see anything... don't worry about it.

Amiria   Must have been a kēhua wandering around, eh Mum? (*giggles*)

Louise   I'm sorry, but I feel so stupid. What's a key-hu-a? What's going on?

Sue/Wai   Nothing to worry about, Lou. (*to* AMIRIA) I told you girl, to shut up. You're not too big for me to give you a clip around the ears, you know.

Rongo   Mum. (*nodding to* LOUISE)

Sue/Wai   (*to* LOUISE) Excuse my eldest daughter – since we've moved to the city she's learnt some bad manners. Hanging around with the wrong people.

Amiria   I think my mother's talking about my boy-friend. That's it, eh Mum? I know you don't like Nick, but he's alright Mum, he's nice to me. Treats me good. Oh, you don't like any-one I know here!

Sue/Wai   Don't you raise your voice at me!

Amiria   I'll do what I like!

Sue/Wai   No you won't!

Amiria	Yes I will, and anyway, Nick and I...
Sue/Wai	You'll what, girl? Eh!?
Amiria	I'll... I'll...
Sue/Wai	(*to* LOUISE) Sorry Lou, for my girl's bad manners.
Amiria	I learnt them from an expert, Mum, from you!
Sue/Wai	You what! You're getting too big for your boots, girl.
Amiria	It's because I need new ones. I've finished. Can I go now!
Sue/Wai	Go!
Amiria	(*leaving*) I'll be down at the beach.

AMIRIA *exits.*

Rongo	Mum, what'd you do that for?
Sue/Wai	(*getting up to leave*) Do what? (*beat*) Now, you finish those. I'll take these to your Dad. I'm sorry you had to see that Louise.

She picks up a basket of food and exits. LOUISE *and* RONGO *work on in silence.* LOUISE *finally breaks it.*

Louise   It's alright. I don't mind. Every family does it. I fought with my father. It's actually the reason I moved here. He thought I was chasing a man. I wasn't. I was leaving one. I didn't tell him that though. I just couldn't stand not being able to have my own voice. Do you know what I mean? *(There is no response from RONGO. LOUISE begins to sing 'The Blue Beat'. It is faint and shaky)* I've heard you have a beautiful voice. I can't sing to save myself, you've probably noticed. *(beat)* You haven't sung since you left home, have you? Boy told me. *(she stumbles)* Why-o-ra. What does it mean? Why-o-ra? *(beat. LOUISE sings 'The Blue Beat')* Seems like all I've done since I got here is sing, ha. *(beat)* Boy said you make the birds blush when you sing; that if he couldn't hear, the thing that he would miss most would be your sweet-sounding voice. That must be something special to have a gift like that. I hope maybe that I can hear it. Maybe?

Rongo   Tē Ūkaipō. The Homeland. That's what Waiora is to us.

Louise   The Homeland.

Rongo   Why did you pick us?

Louise   What?

Rongo   Why did you pick us?

Louise   What?

Rongo   Why did you pick us?

Louise   I, I, I... don't. I didn't pick you. I mean... I saw your mother and Boy at school. I could tell it was his first day. They both looked so lost, like their feet weren't touching the ground, eyes so wide, the way traveller's eyes are on arrival. They looked like the way I felt. I watched them for a while, then came forward and introduced myself. I found out that Boy was in one of my classes. We were both new to this place. Outsiders you see, and it just went from there. So I didn't actually pick you. We kind of chose each other.

Pause.

Rongo   Mum and Amiria are always fighting now. They never used to fight so much at home. *(beat)* I think Mum's real lonely. No one to talk to here; no other whānau, just us.

Louise   Oh, but there's other Māori people here.

Rongo   We're not all the same, you know. We miss *our* family.

Louise   It won't take long. You've only been here a year. You'll get to know people.

Rongo   You don't understand do you?

Louise   Understand what?

Rongo   What we left behind. Back home, if we had a problem, we could go to an aunty, an uncle, and they always knew what to do, but here, we have no one. When we fall, there's no one there to catch us, soften the blow.

Louise   Rongo, you all have work, money, a big house, your father's going to be promoted. You have nothing to fear. Your family's flying high. What are you afraid of?

Rongo   Falling.

BOYBOY *comes rushing in. He is in a frenzy.*

Boyboy   Grab the sacks! Water! We need water! Come quick! Oh hell, the fire for the hāngi! Sparks, up into the scrub and it's burning. Quick! We gotta put it out before Dad comes.

The set becomes the fire. As BOYBOY is ending his speech, the TĪPUNA enter. They begin another haka, 'Tēnā i Tahuna', aimed again at RONGO.

Kaitātaki   *E... i tēnā tahuna...*

Tauā   *Rapahia tonuhia ko te mauri whakatipu wairua tangata e*
tukuna mai, whakaaro tukuna mai raa...
Kia kitea iho ko te pono, ko te tika

Kaitātaki   *Ngaua ana te manawa e!!*

Tauā   *Ai ko te wairangi!!*

Kaitātaki   *Ngaua ana ā roto...*

Tauā   *Whakapōrangi!!*

Kaitātaki   *Ngaua ana ā roto...*

Tauā   *Nā, ko te utu o te whakamau he hāparapara noa i te ngākau e...*
AUĒ HI!![15]

All are vainly trying to put out the fire. HONE enters carrying an assortment of things with him, and begins to fight the fire. Some have water; others sacks. RONGO stands and stares. She sees her tīpuna and they are calling to her. The other characters either retreat into slow motion or are stock still, only to highlight RONGO's isolation. Focus then snaps back to fighting the fire. RONGO is brought back by BOYBOY shaking her. The TĪPUNA are laughing at what they have caused.

Boyboy   Rongo! Rongo! Help! What are you doing?!

The fire is eventually brought under control. The TĪPUNA move to RONGO.

John/Hone   You stupid little bastard. I told you to keep a fucken eye on the fire! Where the hell were you?! Eh?! Where the hell were you?!

[15] See pages 112-113 for English translation.

Boyboy   Down at the beach. You told me to get you some mussels. You said you felt like some. I... I...

John/Hone   (*he strikes at* BOYBOY) Get out of my sight. Go on, get out!

Sue/Wai   (*going to protect* BOYBOY) That's enough! Go on Boy, do as your father says. We'll come and get you when he cools down.

Boyboy   I only wanted to please him.

Sue/Wai   He knows that. Way you go eh, down to the beach.

BOYBOY *exits.*

Louise   I'll go with him.

Sue/Wai   That's a good idea, everything's fine now.

LOUISE *exits.*

John/Hone   No thanks to that bloody Boy. I told you we shouldn't have taken him. He's been trouble right from the start. Give him a chance and he'll cut you. Deep.

Sue/Wai   Baby, you go back and get the rest of the kai. We'll come soon.

RONGO *exits. She is still slightly dazed, looking around in case the* TĪPUNA *have returned. Unseen, the* TĪPUNA *exit with her.* WAI *watches* RONGO *leave. Fury builds between* WAI *and* HONE.

Sue/Wai   Leave that boy alone. He only did it to please you. Let him do that.

John/Hone   I don't want him to please me. I want him to stay away from me.

Sue/Wai   He's got no one else. *(pause)* We took him in, we're his parents.

John/Hone   No we're not. We picked him up, like a stray. We look after him, that's all. I have two daughters and one son.

Sue/Wai   And where is he now ? That one son? Kua mate. *(beat)* You killed him, strangled his spirit and he took off. You're doing it again. Why? Why are you being so hard on him? So he won't turn out like you? You are a good man Hone, but Mahurangi is gone, and you did it. You're the one to blame.

John/Hone   Shut up woman.

Sue/Wai   No, I won't shut up.

John/Hone   What are you trying to say? Go on, tell me what you're thinking! Say it, go on, say it!

Sue/Wai   Alright, you listen to me! I've always been there for you, what you wanted, your dreams. But I have a fire in me and I won't dampen it down, not any more. I have a fire. I lost a son and I hated you for that. You drove our son away and you act like you don't even care, that it was good, and now you turn on Boy and do it again. Why don't you care!?! Why don't you see?!!

John/Hone   I see. I care. (*beat*) When I look at Boy, when I close these hands, when I see your hurt, I care, and I hate myself. It grabs me, holds me down. (*beat*) I know it was me. I closed my hand and I made a fist like this, yeah, like this, and I hit him hard. Boom! My son. He went down, easy. I said 'Mahurangi, that's how my old man dealt with me, with the fist. You gotta learn. I told you not to take the car.' He didn't say nothing. Just got straight back up. He's my boy, you see. He didn't say nothing. That's when I saw it, I dunno what it was or how to... it was... a colour. Between the two of us was a colour, red, ha. Then I said 'You alright boy?' He didn't say nothing. I said 'Ya right boy?' He touched his face, he stood there, stared at me, turned and started to walk. I said 'Come back here!' He didn't take no notice. 'Come back here!' Then that colour, it changed as he walked, from a red to a blue, then from a blue to nothing and he was gone. God, he was gone. (*beat*) I broke him, my own son and I don't think he'll ever be back.

He is shattered. HONE *and* WAI *embrace.*

Sue/Wai   My fire's gone.

John/Hone   I'll try with Boy, I'll try.

The lights fade on them and come up on BOYBOY *alone on the beach. Not far from him, but out of his sight, is* AMIRIA. *She is drinking from a flagon.* BOYBOY *talks to himself, almost mumbling. He thrashes around, revealing his hurt, frustration, anger, finally his sorrow. He sits weeping.* LOUISE *enters and watches.*

Boyboy   Where are you?! He's mad at you, but he takes it out on me. You said... you said you'd always be there for me. Where are you?! You promised, for me. You're not... you're not here! Mahurangi! Hoki mai e te tuakana, hoki mai ki au! Hoki mai![16]

LOUISE *slowly comes into view.*

Louise   Boy. *(pause)* May I?

Boyboy   What do you want?

Louise   Just to sit here, if that's alright?

Boyboy   If you wanna.

Louise   I want to.

Boyboy   I'm sorry for what happened with my whānau.

---

[16] 'Come back to me brother, please come back to me! Come back!'

Louise   At least you have a family who cares about you.

Boyboy   Do I?

Louise   They fight over you.

Boyboy   Did Mum and Dad fight?

Louise   You were there, remember.

Boyboy   It's all my fault. Everything's my fault.

Louise   No it's not. *(beat)* No, it's not.

Boyboy   I wish we were at home; things were good at home.

Louise   Look out here, Boy. It's so beautiful here, isn't that a start?

Boyboy   Not as beautiful as back home.

Louise   That's all I hear, this magical place, Waiora. You make it sound like heaven.

Boyboy   Close to it. We have a mountain that's our heart and the further away from it you get, the weaker you get. Mum said that's why we've been getting sick.

Louise   I'd love to see this mountain.

Boyboy   I'd take you there if I could.

Louise   They'll be 'putting down' the hāngi now.

Boyboy   Hell, I better go. I'm supposed to be doing it.

Louise   Probably too late. Your Dad didn't mind. He said he felt a bit bad really.

Boyboy   He didn't say that.

Louise   You're right, he didn't. He said you had to learn. (*mimicking* HONE's *voice*) 'Boy can get one down next year.' (*laughs*)

Boyboy   Did he say that? Did he really say that? (*beat*) But he knows I'm ready to put one down now! I only wanted to please him, do my best for him.

Louise   You really love your father, don't you?

Boyboy   More than anything.

Louise   Not everyone feels that way about their dad.

Boyboy   Why?

Louise   We have our reasons.

Boyboy   So he's not angry anymore? Na, he will be.

Louise   I can't say.

Pause. The lights change and come up on RONGO *and the* TĪPUNA *entering. The* TĪPUNA *are singing. It is the first few lines of the waiata tangi 'Ko Te Matarekereke'[17]. There is a flash forward.* RONGO *slowly crumples to the ground. As she does, the lights fade on them and come back up on* BOYBOY *and* LOUISE. BOYBOY *and* LOUISE *have seen nothing.* RONGO *and the* TĪPUNA *exit, the tune trailing with them.*

Louise   I can't say. (*beat*) Who's Mahurangi?

Boyboy   Why?

Louise   I heard you before, calling out to him.

Boyboy   Did you? (*beat*) He's my older brother.

Louise   Where is he?

Pause.

Boyboy   No one knows. He took off about a year ago.

Louise   Oh, how come?

Boyboy   He has his reasons.

Louise   It sounds like you miss him a lot.

Boyboy   More than that. He was always there for me. (*beat*) I better go, eh.

[17] See full waiata page 104.

BOY *moves to go.*

Louise   Hold on, there's something I want to ask you.

Boyboy   Ahhh...

Louise   Have you told your father about school? About being suspended?

Boyboy   What about it?

Louise   You know what I mean.

Boyboy   Yeah, he knows.

Louise   Are you lying to me?

Boyboy   No. Why do you think he was so mad with me before? It wasn't only the fire. Still a bit hot about school. It's alright now though.

Louise   And your Mum?

Boyboy   Yeah, she knows.

AMIRIA, *who has been listening to all of this, makes some noise.* LOUISE *and* BOYBOY *discover her there. She is drunk. She holds a half-empty flagon in her hand.*

Amiria   Ho, ho, ho and a Merry Christmas!! *(laughing. To* BOYBOY) So Mum and Dad know eh? All about our little brother being naughty at school? *(laughs again)*

Boyboy	(*under his breath*) Please don't tell them.
Louise	Amiria, are you drunk?
Amiria	Drunk? No, us Maoris put on this show for you Pākehā fullas all the time. (*laughing*) I'm sure you would have seen it before. Let me do a bit of a dance for ya. (*she dances a satirical haka, pokes out her tongue*) Yeah, I'm drunk alright.
Louise	We'll take her back to your parents.
Boyboy	No.
Louise	Well you can't leave her here.
Boyboy	Yeah, you go back, tell them we're on our way. We went for a walk.
Louise	I don't want to lie to your parents.
Boy	She'll get a hiding if she goes back like this.
Louise	I'll go back, but I won't lie.
Boyboy	You won't be, if you say we're on our way, 'cause we will be. Please Miss Stones. (*pause; she hesitates, then nods*) Thank you Miss Stones, thank you.
Amiria	Yes, thank you Miss Stones. (giggles)

53

Louise   (*to* BOYBOY) I know you're lying. You tell them, or I will.

LOUISE *exits. Lights fade on* AMIRIA *and* BOYBOY *as they exit. They then come up on* HONE, WAI, RONGO *and* STEVE CAMPBELL, *Hone's boss, the long-awaited guest. He is in his late thirties, dressed for the occasion, wears a hat and jacket and obviously is a little awkward.* HONE *pours him a beer.*

Sue/Wai   So you found the place alright, Mr Campbell?

Steve   Steve, please.

Sue/Wai   Alright, Steve.

Steve   Yes, took me a while. Don't usually come out this way.

John/Hone   We only found it by accident. Was looking for a good place to go diving for pāua, kina.

Steve   Kina?

John/Hone   Yeah kina, spiny things. Like hedgehogs.

Steve   Oh yes.

John/Hone   Anyway, we found this place.

Steve   It's beaut.

Sue/Wai   Thank you for coming, Steve.

Steve   Couldn't really say no. John was on at me
                       most of the week. He said your steam pud-
                       ding was something not to be missed.

John/Hone   Steve, I'd just like to say that it's really good
                       to have you here today. To come all this way,
                       when you didn't have to. I want to thank you
                       for coming on behalf of me and my family.
                       It's a real... honour eh, to have you at my girl's
                       birthday. Thanks and welcome.

Sue/Wai   (leaning over to HONE) Do you want us to
                       sing?

John/Hone   No, Jesus!

Steve   (a little embarrassed) The thanks should come
                       from me, thanking you for inviting me. (beat)
                       So, is this the birthday girl?

Sue/Wai   Yes, this is our youngest girl. 18 today.

Though he isn't doing it intentionally, Steve should be crowding
RONGO. RONGO *is dominated by this new arrival.*

Steve   Not a girl, a woman. (chuckles) Rongo, isn't
                       it?

Rongo   (prodded by her mother) Yes.

Steve   Well, ah, Happy Birthday Rongo. I thought
                       since this was a birthday I should bring a gift.
                       (he hands her a package)

Sue/Wai	You shouldn't have.
Steve	It's not much, eh.
Sue/Wai	Oh Steve.
Steve	No, it's not.
John/Hone	Well, thank the man.
Rongo	Thank you Mr Campbell.
Steve	Steve, please.
Rongo	Steve.

LOUISE *enters.*

Steve	I know you jokers start a bit earlier than us, but this can't be another one of your daughters? *(laughing)*
John/Hone	This is our youngest son's school teacher. Mr Steve Campbell, Miss Louise Stones.
Louise	Good to meet you.
Steve	And you.

Pause.

Louise	Your wife couldn't come?

Steve   Not married. No one wants me. (*laughs; they all join in*)

WAI *keeps laughing; no one else does.*

Sue/Wai   Where's Amiria and Boy?

Louise   Oh, they're on their way.

Steve   That's who was missing, Amiria. She's a one that one. Always on the go at smoko. Solid though, good worker like her old man.

Sue/Wai   I don't think we've thanked you for getting her that job. She's thrilled with it.

Steve   No problem. It's great to know people are happy at work. Like I said, the only reason she got it is because of her Dad. (*beat; to* LOUISE) I don't think I've see you round here?

Louise   (*distracted*) No, from further south.

Steve   Whereabouts?

Louise   Winton. Central Southland.

Steve   Yeah, I know where that is. A Southlander. How come you left?

Louise   Wanted to spread my wings and see the world.

Steve　　　Well, this part of the South Island ain't the world, but it's a good start. Ain't that right John?

John/Hone　　Oh yeah. It's not the East Coast, mind you, but it will do.

Steve　　　That right?

Sue/Wai　　Oh, it's beautiful there.

Steve　　　Is that why they call it Poverty Bay then? (*laughs*)

John/Hone　　That's what you call it. (*laughs*)

Sue/Wai　　Beer Steve?

Steve　　　Yep, don't mind if I do.

Louise　　So you run the mill?

Steve　　　I do now. Took over from the old man. 'Iron fist', we call him. It's been ours since the turn of the century, got it off the locals. My grandfather said they didn't have a clue. They'd only cut down a few, enough for themselves. Ha, how the hell are ya gonna make any money carrying on like that? Still, Maoris some of the best workers I got, like John here. This bloke knows his stuff. Brought him down cause he knows timber. How to cut the logs right, get the most out of it. He'll look at a log, like that tree over there. Outta that, he'll get a couple of three-inch, six two-inch and an inch and a quarter on either side. This man has vision. It was a bit of a risk bringing him down, but by god, it's paid off and he's gonna be duly rewarded for it.

John/Hone   Thank you, Steve.

Steve   Don't mention it. *(beat)* But let's not get into talking about work in front of the women.

Louise   Yes, let's not talk about work. *(beat)* Is there anything else for me to do?

Sue/Wai   Anything else, Louise you're so funny sometimes. Don't worry about doing anything, leave it all up to us.

Louise   No, no just point me and I'll go and do it. I'm your slave.

Sue/Wai   Slave. *(laughs)* Don't joke like that Louise. You're our guest, like Steve.

Steve   Stones? Stones? *(beat)* This might be a long shot, but you any relative to Godfrey Stones down there?

Louise   Um yes, he's my father.

Steve   What the hell are you doing here? A school teacher?

Louise   I wanted to get away. I like teaching.

Sue/Wai   What is it? Is there something you haven't told us, Lou?

Louise   It's nothing really.

Steve   Nothing? Only that Lou here, I should say Louise, is loaded. She's the daughter of one of the richest men in New Zealand. Wanted to see how the rest of us lived, eh? Can't get much closer than John and his family. Me, for that matter. Hell, Godfrey Stones.

Sue/Wai   (*noticing* LOUISE *and how uncomfortable she is*) Rongo, you haven't opened your present yet.

Steve   No you haven't. Go ahead, it won't bite you.

She opens it carefully. It is soap.

Steve   Don't you like it?

Rongo   Thank you Mr Campbell.

Steve   Do you like it? You don't do ya? Soap, soap. (*beat*) I didn't mean it to be rude or anything.

Louise   Rude?

Sue/Wai   She likes it. Of course she likes it. It's a lovely present. (*to* RONGO) Say thank you.

Rongo   Thank you Mr Campbell.

BOYBOY *and* AMIRIA *enter. They are soaked. They stay far enough away from* HONE *and* WAI *and the others so as not to be seen.* AMIRIA *is still very drunk.* BOYBOY *is trying vainly to keep her quiet. They overhear everything.*

Steve   Whew, thank you Sue. That's alright then, eh. I'm glad that the birthday girl liked it, she's what counts. *(beat)* I heard that you were a bit of a singer or so your old man said. How about a song from the birthday girl? *(beat)* That is if it's alright with your Mum and Dad. He said your voice is, ah, how did he put it? 'Heaven-sent!'

John/Hone   Sure is eh! No, that's not a problem is it Baby? Heaven-sent, where's the gat? *(he goes to look for it)* She loves singing. Can't shut her up half the time. Sing, sing, sing.

Sue/Wai   Come on Baby, it's the least you can do, since Steve brought you a present. How about 'Hine e hine'?

John/Hone   Ah... Waiata i roto i te reo Pākehā.[18]

Sue/Wai   Oh yes, of course. Come on baby.

Rongo   Please, Mum.

Steve   Oh, don't worry, I didn't mean it to be a big thing.

[18] 'Sing something in English'

John/Hone	Eh? Has the cat got your tongue? (*laughs; he strums some chords of the song*) How about this one? Rongo?! Baby, or this one?!
Rongo	(*she tries to sing, but nothing comes out*) I, I, I... can't.
John/Hone	(*under his breath*) Just sing, Baby. For me.
Rongo	(*almost in tears*) I can't Dad.

She just stands there. AMIRIA has had enough. She moves to save her sister. She breaks free from BOYBOY and comes forward. LOUISE sees her first.

Amiria	I'll sing.
Louise	Amelia, I don't think that's...
Steve	(*turning*) Yeah, that's OK. Don't worry... (*sees that she is soaking wet*) ...about it.

HONE, WAI *and* LOUISE *freeze. They obviously know that* AMIRIA *is drunk.* STEVE *doesn't yet realise.* HONE *and* WAI *are too stunned to reply.*

Amiria	Hello Mr Campbell. (*she almost curtsies*)
Steve	You're soaked through.
Amiria	Oh am I? I slipped, fell into a bit of a hole. (*laughs*)

62

Steve   Did your brother fall in the same one?

Amiria   Was a big hole. (*laughs*) I'll sing for you. What
                 do you want? I know heaps of really good
                 ones. Dad likes Elvis Presley, don't you Dad?

Sue/Wai   Bub, come and get dried off eh?

Amiria   Mum, it's alright, it's hot. I'm on fire. I'll dry
                 off real quick. (*beat*) I'll sing for you, Mr
                 Campbell. I'm not as good a singer as my
                 sister, not heaven sent, not me, not Amelia.
                 (*beat*) Does my father ever talk about me? No?
                 What a surprise. No, I don't suppose you ever
                 heard my Dad talk about me. But I'll sing for
                 you. To thank you for what you've done for
                 this family, for giving me a job. (*to* HONE) A
                 song? Oh yes, yes, yes I've got it. Don't worry,
                 not a Māori one. (*beat*) You see, my sister used
                 to sing all the time, that's true, but she hasn't
                 since we got here. She says she can't, so she
                 can't. But I'll sing for you, yes I'll sing for
                 you, Mr Campbell.

AMIRIA *starts to sing 'Till We Kissed'. Her rendition of the song
becomes too much – it is lewd and suggestive toward* STEVE.
WAI *finally gets up enough courage to stop it.*

Sue/Wai   Kāti! Kāti! Kōtiro pōrangi.[19]

Louise   That's ah, beautiful Amiria, but that's enough
                 now, eh?

[19] 'Stop it! Stop it! You stupid girl'

Sue/Wai   (*turns to* LOUISE) Beautiful, that's not beautiful. Kei te aha koe. Ko whakamā tō pāpā me
ahau i a koe.[20]

Louise   I didn't mean that, I meant...

AMIRIA *stops.*

Amiria   Oh, I'm sorry Mr Campbell, it looks like this
is the end of my song. But just remember
Steve, I'll sing for you whenever you want.

They exit. HONE *is left, with* BOYBOY *still dripping wet.*
RONGO *has gone closer to her father.*

John/Hone   Steve, I don't...

Steve   Don't worry about it. Ah, these things happen. Kids get drunk. (*beat*) Ya know, I can
remember the first time I got plastered in front
of my parents. Hell, did I get a... It's a mistake. I'm sure you've made some, John?

John/Hone   (*measured*) Yeah I have.

Steve   Well then, let's forget about it eh?

John/Hone   Sure. (*pause*) Boy, get out of those clothes.

Boyboy   Yes Dad. (*he exits*)

John/Hone   (*out*) Boy, after you done that, go and check
on the hāngi. Make sure no steam's coming
out. Ya hear me?! That's your job!

---

[20]'Look, what you are doing?! You're hurting your father. You're hurting me'

Boyboy   (*offstage*) Yeah Dad.

John/Hone   Rongo, go and see if your Mum needs a hand, eh? (*she doesn't move*) Go on. (*She exits.*) (*offering* STEVE *a beer*) Steve?

Steve   (*skulls back the glass*) Thanks. (*pause*) How much longer with the hāngi?

John/Hone   'Bout an hour and a half, I reckon.

Steve   That long.

John/Hone   You can go if you like. I don't blame ya.

Steve   What for?

John/Hone   That thing with girl.

Steve   What thing? It was a mistake. (*beat*) I'm hungry, can't wait. I came to have a feed with you and your family and I'll do that. (*beat*) Your kids'll be alright. Teething problems. Nobody feels good in a new place. (*beat*) Me, I was born here; it's home, part of me. Three generations of Campbells have lifted their eyes to this place. Three. One of the first to come here. Started with nothing. Just like you. (*beat*) Ya spend enough time anywhere and the place'll own ya, take ya over. This place owns me and my family. My grandfather's buried here, so we're always part of it now. The land. When I look out, see the mountains, the hills, I see him. *(beat)* We were farmers before we got into timber. It's the land, ya understand that... the bond with the land. It's home when ya work the land.

John/Hone   I understand. Thanks.

Steve   Don't mention it. *(beat)* Those kids'll come round.

John/Hone   Yeah, they will. *(pause)* Steve, I want to...

Steve   Don't worry about it mate, let's just drink eh? *(beat)* Look, I got something for you. Was gonna save it for later, but well, ya probably knew it was coming anyway and it's not 'cause I'm a decent joker. There's a reason for it John. In the last couple of months we've been having record cuts, record. Cutting twice as many logs as we used to and you're the reason mate, the best bloke I've ever had on the head rig. The best. Sure there isn't sap in your veins? *(laughs)*

John/Hone   Na. *(chuckles)* Maybe a bit too much of the old brown stuff.

Steve   Too right. I can see we're gonna have a bloody good future. Hey, soon we'll have your whole family working at the mill.

John/Hone   No! I brought my kids here for a better life, Steve. I appreciate what you've done for us, for me, but I don't want my kids working at the mill. I'm bloody proud of what I do and I'm good at it, and I know Amiria's there in the office, but I want better for my kids. I don't want them to ever do what we did, me and my wife. We did things people shouldn't have to do. (*beat*) We came here for a better life, not the same one.

Steve   Well, I reckon what I've got for ya will definitely help along the way.

John/Hone   I'm sure it will. It's good work Steve, hard. Maybe there is sap in these veins. I'd miss it if I didn't have any work, be able to use these. (*indicates his hands*) Be like a baby, helpless. Jeez, I'd hate that.

Steve   Yeah, wouldn't know what to do with myself if I had too much time. (*to self*) Maybe that's why I push so hard. (*to* HONE) Ya know John, we're the same in so many ways, believe we can make things better, for you, for your family; me, well, for me, and all from working in a sawmill. (*beat*) People, outsiders, they come into the mill, they look down on us, they stop, they stare, they hear noise, smell dust, see blokes 'carting timber'. But that's all they see. They don't see what we're trying to do. I've worked everywhere in that place, from outside stripping to running the head rig myself. I know hard work, so do you, that's why we're gonna be together for a long time. We understand each other see. We understand what helps to make things... better. You're a tower of strength, John. *(beat)* You pushed us along, so I want to reward you... actually...

John/Hone   Eh?!

Steve   I just thought, not yet, I should wait till ya whole family's here. Can't have good news falling only on your ears. Need the family.

John/Hone   Yeah, need the family.

Steve   Don't feel too bad about the kids, they'll come round. I envy you John, I really do. You have a family, someone to care for, someone who will care about you. Me, I have my work. I was thinkin' the other day, how come I'm always at do's like this? Saying 'yes', I real- ised it's because I want ah... I want what you have, a family. Care for them John, don't ever let them go. *(he is embarrassed by his frank- ness; he breaks away)* Hey, since it looks like we'll be in for a long haul, I'll nip back to the car, get a couple more jars. Wasn't too sure if this was a drinking do or not.

John/Hone   Yep, that sounds bonza.

Steve   Well, I'll see ya in the shake of a dog's leg.

STEVE *exits. Hone is left alone. He looks and watches as* STEVE *leaves. He contemplates what has just been said, rolls it around in his mind and finally explodes.*

John/Hone   Yes! Yes! You bloody beauty! Tower of strength, he said! Tower of strength! Whoo hoo! *(he breaks into 'Takupatu Auē', dancing to it)* Kei te tika koe, Mum. Kei te tika. Kei te haere pai ngā mea katoa ki a ahau. Āe, e mum. Kei te pai![21] *(beat)* Hone mate, looks like you made the right choice, waited for your Mum to pass away, then brought your whānau south. 'Too late', they said. 'Kids almost grown up.' Na! Stuff you! *(laughs)* Foreman. Yeah, things are looking up. I knew it, I knew it. If I just worked hard, things would happen, and they are, they bloody are. *(beat)* I've got a lot to thank Steve for. Right from the word go, he looked out for me. When that joker wouldn't let me in the social club, 'Can't have no Maoris' he said, I wanted to drop the bastard. Steve stepped in and that was it. Now the promotion, and he wants to make it more special by telling me in front of my whānau. He tino pai tēnei rā! What a great day!

Lights slowly fade on him. The TĪPUNA *come forward and sing the waiata 'Taukuri e'. Lights fade. End of Act 1.*

---

[21] 'You were right Mum, you were right. Things will go my way and they have. They have Mum, they have!'

Act 2

Mid-afternoon. It is not long after the hāngi has been lifted. Everyone has eaten. Most of the dishes have been cleared away, but there is a sprinkling still around. An ill-ease still pervades the air. HONE, still embarrassed at AMIRIA's display, plies STEVE with alcohol. The children sit around attentively, RONGO close to her father, AMIRIA playing cards by herself. BOYBOY and AMIRIA are dressed in old clothes, AMIRIA in her father's bush shirt and shorts, BOYBOY in shorts and singlet.

John/Hone   Steve. Another?

Before he is able to answer, BOYBOY is there to fill up his glass.

Steve   Of course. Well trained eh? Thank you John, I ah, don't mind if I do. *(beat)* I have to say Sue, that John wasn't exaggerating about your steam pudding. Beaut, just beaut. If you weren't married to John, I'd go after ya myself. *(chuckles)*

Sue/Wai   Oh Steve, you're a card. We've got more, if you want. Plenty more. Amiria.

Steve   No. No. Thanks. You're killing me with kindness. Not that I deserve it. Thanks anyway. I'm as full as a bull. *(laughs)* It's a great way to hold on to ya guests eh? Is that how you nailed down John? Fill him up so he couldn't move?

Sue/Wai   Well no, it wasn't, eh... John?

The STRANGER *enters.* RONGO *recognises the* STRANGER
immediately as one of the TĪPUNA. *She looks around to see if
any of the others have noticed the new arrival. She's relieved
when everyone has. The* STRANGER *carries a bag. They all
stop.* HONE *and* WAI *rise.*

John/Hone   Gidday. Come in.

Stranger   Thank you.

He offers the STRANGER *a seat. It is politely refused. The*
STRANGER *is quietly wary of them.*

Steve   You're a long way from anything – going
diving?

Stranger   Searching for strays.

Steve   Sheep?

Stranger   Lost ones. (*the* STRANGER *notices* RONGO's
unwrapped present) A party? Didn't mean to
get in the way.

Sue/Wai   You're not. Yes, a birthday for our daughter,
Rongo.

Stranger   Happy birthday, may this be a day you will
never forget.

Rongo   Thank you.

Sue/Wai	Are you hungry?
Stranger	Yes. Been a long day already and I have such a journey back. Brought nothing with me. Didn't think I would be away for so long.
Sue/Wai	We have plenty – sit, eat. You're more than welcome.
Stranger	Thank you, but I have so much to do. I have others to meet up with. The day will be coming to an end soon.
Sue/Wai	Well, take some with you. (*she gathers up some left-over food, wraps it with a tea towel and gives it to the* STRANGER) For the journey back, for all of you. (*hands over the food; it is accepted*)
Stranger	Kia ora. I feel I should give you something. (*looks about for something to give*) But I have nothing.
John/Hone	That's more than enough then isn't it? Look, we have plenty.
Stranger	You're very kind. (*beat*) I better get going. Goodbye, and thank you. (*turns to* RONGO) Goodbye Rongo.
Rongo	Bye. (*the* STRANGER *turns to go*) Wait! Be careful when you get to the end of the beach. The rocks are sharp and the land is uneven, you

might hurt yourself if you don't watch out.
There's a track through it – I could show you
if you want. *(she looks to her mother and father; they nod)*

Stranger   Thank you, but I know the track, I've been
there before.

Rongo   Oh, I could still show you.

Stranger   You should stay here with your family.
Goodbye.

Louise   Good luck.

Stranger   Thank you.

The STRANGER *exits. They watch as the* STRANGER *leaves.*

Steve   Well, that's one visitor you couldn't hold on
to, eh Sue?

Sue/Wai   True, very true Steve, and that doesn't happen
very often.

RONGO *stays staring out to the distance. Everyone else gets
back to the day. Drinks refilled, the pause with the* STRANGER
quickly forgotten. The focus shifts back to STEVE.

Steve   I'm sure it doesn't. *(beat)* Now how did you
and John get together? You were about to tell
us before.

John/Hone   Oh, just the usual, ya know, met each other at a dance.

Amiria   (*quickly*) No it wasn't. Our Dad was a bit of a hero, eh Dad?

John/Hone   What?!

Louise   A hero? Tell us more.

Steve   Yeah, come on mate, this is something I didn't expect. (*beat*) What ya do – save her from drowning or something?

John/Hone   Oh, was nothing eh, was pretty stupid.

Louise   The more reason to hear about it. Sue?

Sue/Wai   Oh he's right, it wasn't much.

Steve   It must be something for the two of you to hold back so much. Come on Sue, I know we won't get it out of ya old man.

Louise   Yeah, come on Sue.

Amiria   (*chuckling*) Yeah, come on Sue!

Sue/Wai   (*to* HONE) Shall I?

John/Hone   May as well, cause we'll never hear the end of it, until ya do.

Sue/Wai   Well... well, he picked me up, eh. Real, like he picked me up. Yeah.

The TĪPUNA *begin to quietly sing 'The Tennessee Waltz' in the background.* WAI *begins to giggle. The kids join in the fun as the story is told.*

John/Hone   Get on with it, woman.

Sue/Wai   Oh sorry. Well, we have this one picture house in Waiora. It's really just the local hall eh, shows films and stuff. Well, we hadn't even started going out, he was too shy I thought.

Rongo   Too shy, eh Dad!

Sue/Wai   Not like now. Saw each other at local dances and things. We knew we liked each other cause our friends kept telling us, but jeez, he was so shy he never even asked me to dance or nothing. Always stayed glued to the wall, with his checked suit and slicked black hair – half a jar I reckon, looking like some wonky tukutuku panel. So clean and smart.

Rongo/Amiria   *(say this line with their mother)* 'So clean and smart.' *(they giggle)*

Sue/Wai   You two! *(beat)* Well anyway, at the end of one of the dances I had had enough. I went up to him and said 'I'm going to the flicks next week. It's a John Wayne movie, *Tall in the Saddle*, I'll see ya there', and left.

(*she giggles*) I turned up at the movie and he was nowhere to be seen. I thought I scared him off. I was really angry. We sat down, me and my cousin Missy. I was thinking (RONGO *and* AMIRIA *again join in*) 'That Hone, I'll give him what for when I see him.' (*they laugh*) The movie was on and John Wayne was rockin' and rollin', getting the bad guys, Pow! Pow! I'd almost forgotten about him. Then, all of a sudden the hall was filled with light. Everyone turned round and at the door was Hone, on horseback, dressed like John Wayne. I didn't know what he was gonna do – no one did. People were yahooing, chucking stuff, lollies, chairs going, oh it was such a hooha. He comes riding down the aisle yelling, 'Wai, Wai, where the hell are ya? Wai?!' I tried to hide, but my cousin called back, 'Over here, over here!' The next thing, he shot down, scooped me up. Well, everyone let out a big cheer, it was just like the movies, and we rode outta there, the hall caretaker yelling at us, 'You two come back here, come back. I know who you are! I know your parents!' (*beat*) We got banned from the flicks for ages after that, but I didn't care, I had my man.

Steve   (*laughing*) Who would have thought, eh? Horses! Scooped up! John Wayne! Oh that's great, that's great!

Louise   John, I would never have guessed.

John/Hone   (*embarrassed*) Oh hell, I... oh, it was stupid, eh. I don't know. Oh jeez.

Steve   (*laughing*) Oh my puku.

Boyboy   Mum's too good a cook, eh Mr Campbell? Couldn't help yourself.

Steve   Yep, too right, couldn't help myself, and call me Steve. Please.

Boyboy   Yeah sorry.

Steve   No need to be sorry. (*beat*) Every time I get together with your mob, I've always got the same complaint.

Louise   Complaint?! What are you talking about?!

Steve   Keep ya britches on. The complaint is that you people always try to feed me to death, and if that doesn't work you try and make me laugh myself to death. (*beat*) Do I look that scrawny? (*laughs*) Who was it the last time? That's right – Tommy Rahui and his mob, almost did the same thing. Not a bad way to go though.

John/Hone   I wouldn't mind going that way, as long as they chucked in a big bag of kinas. (*laughs*)

Steve   Kinas.

Boyboy   I wouldn't mind going that way either! (*laughing*) Āe, he kete kina. Tino reka.[22]

Sue/Wai   Boy.

Boyboy   (*still laughing at his own joke*) Yeah Mum.

Sue/Wai   That's enough, eh!

Louise   (*quickly*) John says things have been going well at the mill, Steve?

Steve   Going well?! Booming, more like it. Might even have to get in more staff. (*beat*) Get a couple of John's family down from up north. If they're all like him we can't lose. All this building around the city, ya see. They need timber and we've got it. Just got a deal to buy more land, plant more trees. Oh, it's there for the picking. (*to* HONE) John, where does a man go to talk to a dog?

John/Hone   Just over there by those trees.

Steve   Oh. Oh well, do as the locals do... If you'll excuse me.

He exits.

John/Hone   (*to* BOYBOY) Come here! Keep your bloody mouth shut, eh. We've had enough trouble today and I don't want it getting any worse with you shooting your mouth off, and you,

---

[22] 'A bag of kina. Yummy.'

(*to* AMIRIA) get your lip off the bloody ground before I do it for you and get over here. (*to* WAI) Jesus, control these kids will ya! Only my baby here's (*indicating* RONGO) helping out her Dad.

Louise   John, don't you think you're being a little bit harsh. I don't think Steve minds in the slightest. He's having a good time.

Sue/Wai   Ah, Lou.

Louise   Yes Sue?

Sue/Wai   Can you come over here?

Louise   Sure, anything you want.

Sue/Wai   Boy, the water should be hot now, put it in the basin and bring it here.

BOYBOY *exits. They separate from* RONGO, HONE *and* AMIRIA, *taking with them dishes.*

Louise   So, what can I do for you Sue?

Sue/Wai   You are my friend, right? And we can talk to each other?

Louise   Of course. Of course.

Sue/Wai   Well, you're getting out of line.

Louise   Oh, I, I, I don't understand. What do you mean?

Sue/Wai   I just don't want you to talk to my husband like that.

Louise   Sue, I didn't mean to interfere. But everyone's behaving so strangely since Steve turned up, everyone's changed. You started treating me like you had just met me. Steve is fine. You treated that stranger better than you're treating me. I don't understand why John is being so hard on the kids. I just don't understand.

Sue/Wai   Please try. Just trust us. I'm sorry Lou, but my husband is the head of this family. He may not do everything right in your eyes and he may not run it, but he is still the head. So I want you to show him that respect. *(beat)* Everything, I mean everything has changed for us, this place, having to learn your ways.

Louise   You don't have to do that at all. No one's making you. If it's that hard I'll look after you.

Sue/Wai   No you won't. Were you listening to me just now? We are not your pets. We are people and you should treat us that way. When we speak or do things our way, people make fun of us, mock us. Even my children put us down. All we can fight for is our children's respect. John deserves that much and I'll make

sure he gets it, especially today. *(beat)* So I'm
sorry Lou, if we treat you differently when
Steve is there, but you are our guest, our guest,
and we are only returning you respect.

BOYBOY *enters with the basin of water.*

Just put it down over there, son. Thank you.
(beat) Do as your father says, eh?

Boyboy   Āe, Mum.

John/Hone   You girls, go and help your Mum with the
dishes eh?

RONGO *and* AMIRIA *go over to their mother.* BOYBOY *sits
near his father.*

Sue/Wai   *(to* LOUISE*)* Leave the dishes to me, please.
You're our guest. Please.

Louise   Sure.

STEVE *returns and sits near* HONE. LOUISE *comes over to
them. Lights come back up on the three.*

Steve   It's a beautiful place here, eh? You could do
a lot with it. That land over there – you could
pick it up for a song. Burn it off, plant pine
and 30 years time, you could mill it. Make a
fortune.

John/Hone   That's a great idea.

Steve	There you have it again. That's the difference between you and me, and Maoris in general, ya see.
John/Hone	Anyone could see it's a good idea.
Steve	But from the Maoris I know, they'd probably get up there on that hill and watch the sunset. Now what use is there in that? They're gonna have to change, learn to take the opportunity.
John/Hone	We will.
Steve	I'll wait to see it...

There is a pause.

Steve	I thought you had another son? Where is he?
John/Hone	Yeah, we do. Our eldest son, Mahurangi (*looking to* BOYBOY) He's up north.
Steve	Oh right, what does he do up north?
John/Hone	He's... ah, working in an office, ah insurance and stuff.
Steve	Insurance, what type of insurance?
Louise	(*jumping in*) Life insurance, isn't it John?
John/Hone	(*taken aback*) Ah, yeah.

Steve	Oh, I might have to get in touch with him. Get him to have a look at my policy. The old body here's getting a bit tired. (*beat*) Isn't he the one you said was a gun footballer?
John/Hone	Yeah, could go all the way if he really tried.
Louise	Boy here's a really good footballer, aren't you Boy?
John/Hone	He's alright. Not as good as Mahurangi.
Steve	I bet you're just as good, aren't ya?
Boyboy	(*looking to his father*) I'm alright.
Steve	What position? You a back? No. Ya sure? Ya can't be a lock, don't look like a prop, so you must be a wing-forward. What's the flash new name for it now?
Boyboy	Breakaway.
Steve	Breakaway! That's it. (*beat*) So who's ya idol then, eh? Kel Tremain? Wilson Whineray?
Boyboy	Nah.
Steve	Who then?
Boyboy	Waka Nathan.

Steve	Ah, the Black Panther. Stick to your own eh? By jeez, he's a good one though, isn't he? Bit flash. Me, I like the way the All Blacks play nothing fancy, but they win the games.
John/Hone	*(begins to speak, then stops himself)* Yeah, bu...
Boyboy	Yeah, but we haven't lost a game for ages. Eh Dad?

HONE *nods.*

Steve	That may be true, but it's not that you win. It's how you win. You throw the ball around willy-nilly and there's no pattern to it. You don't know if you're gonna win or lose, but with the Blacks there's always a pattern, a game plan, and there's a bigger chance they'll win.
Boyboy	But it's exciting to watch. Waka Nathan plays better in the Maoris than the All Blacks. Dad says that all the time.
John/Hone	Boy.
Steve	Na, na, he's alright. It makes him a fancy player, not a well disciplined one. Ya see son, it's like the difference between me and ya Dad. Well, maybe not ya Dad, but Maoris and us. We're running this country and pretty well, because we've stuck to the basics, a game plan. Stop me if you think I'm going too far.

John/Hone   No, no. You're spot on.

Steve   Where was I? Yeah, if you run the country, to be honest, it'd be a bit of a shambles. Since we got here, we've been building this place for a better future. That's why ya Mum and Dad came here. They could see there was no future in the old ways. You wait – when you have kids and when they have kids, they'll thank us for the effort we put in. Isn't that right, Lou?

Louise   Oh yes, I'm sure they'll have something to say about it.

Steve   Hell, we were talking about rugby, how'd we get onto that?

John/Hone   Dunno, maybe it's the beer talking.

Steve   Maybe. (*he picks up one of* BOY's *gumboots*) Here, show me what you're made of...

He tosses it to BOYBOY. *The two begin to toss it around.* STEVE *begins to commentate.* HONE *sits,* LOUISE *is enjoying the situation.* RONGO, AMIRIA *and* WAI *return.*

Steve   ...he hands off to Nathan, fends off one and another, oh, what grace, what style. Listen for it! Listen! He's over! It's a try! (*laughing*)

He passes it again to BOYBOY. *This time,* BOYBOY *stumbles and knocks into his father, spilling his drink over him. There is immediate silence.*

Steve   Oh, oh sorry 'bout that John. Don't blame the boy. I was the one leading him on, playing the fool.

John/Hone   *(pause)* Yeah, lucky we weren't inside, eh? *(laughs)*

Steve   Refill and drink.

There is relief. RONGO refills their beers.

Steve   I'm puffed, lost my breath for a moment there.

Sue/Wai   *(to* LOUISE*)* Have I missed out on anything?

Louise   Not much. Steve was just doing a bit of fortune telling.

Sue/Wai   *(aside to* LOUISE*)* Has he said anything about the promotion?

Louise   Nothing, not a word.

Sue/Wai   Not even a hint?

Louise   Not even that.

Sue/Wai   Is there anything I can get you Steve? Louise?

Steve   No thanks Sue, the amber liquid will do nicely at the moment.

Louise	Same thanks.
Sue/Wai	Sure. We'll have the cake soon. And Rongo's present.
Steve	I'm sure it will be absolutely bonza Sue. Absolutely beaut! (*laughs*) Come on there John, you're dragging the chain.
John/Hone	Just drinking to a pattern.
Steve	(*to* HONE) Presents, surprise.
Amiria	Dad, can I go to...
John/Hone	No you can't.
Sue/Wai	(*to* LOUISE) Why doesn't he say anything?
Louise	Why don't I try and get it out of him?
Sue/Wai	How?
Louise	Womanly charms? Please let me do that.
Sue/Wai	I don't know. (*pause*) Well, okay – we've got to know. (*beat*)
Steve	Look Sue. Sue, you should sit down. You've been up all day.
Sue/Wai	I enjoy it.

Steve   Does she ever sit down?

Louise   Oh Steve, I was wondering if you'd seen any of this area before, like the beach and things?

Steve   No, unless you count from behind that tree over there? (*laughs*)

Louise   I've been down to the beach. I could show you. I mean, I'm so full, I could do with a walk. That's if it's okay with you John – both your guests disappearing for a while.

Amiria   Will you need a chaperone? (*giggles*)

Steve   Oh, I umm, I don't think so.

Louise   She was joking. John?

John/Hone   Oh yeah, fine eh. We can keep busy here.

Louise   Sure?

John/Hone   Sure.

Louise   Steve?

Steve   Can't turn down the invitation of a lady. Especially a rich one. (*laughs*)

Louise   Certainly not. See you soon then.

LOUISE *exits,* STEVE *rather sheepishly behind her. Everyone says goodbye – 'See you soon', 'Later'. They all relax.*

John/Hone   (*making sure they've gone*) What the hell was all that about?

Amiria   Jeez! She's a fast worker.

John/Hone   Be quiet girl, you keep getting cheeky and you'll go for another swim. (*to* WAI) Why did she take him away? Does she like him?

Sue/Wai   Maybe she does. Maybe she doesn't.

LOUISE *and* STEVE *enter and are lit. They are walking along the beach. The others on stage freeze.* LOUISE *and* STEVE *may be able to move through the others or stay in the same spot.*

Steve   They're a bloody funny bunch, aren't they? John's mob. He's a good bloke though, not like other Maoris I met. Hard worker, not afraid to get his hands dirty. Jeez, but they're a funny bunch, aren't they? (*beat*) Okay, so why did you ask me here? It's certainly not because I'm the most handsome man in the world.

Louise   No.

Steve   Well, what is it?

Louise   I wanted to find out about John's promotion.

Steve   (*laughs*) Promotion! Oh, now it makes sense. Not so green, are ya?

Louise   Nope, so when are you gonna tell him?

Steve   So that's what he thinks is gonna happen. I only got a bonus for him. *(he takes it out of his pocket)* I thought that's what he'd want the most – money.

Louise   But they all think...

Steve   Look, I'd love to. Like I said, John's a good bloke. Works hard. But he's wrong. I can't let a Māori be in charge. It was a battle to get him in the social club. The bloody social club! *(beat)* Look, we all know our places. John and Sue do, I do. Maybe in time those places will change, but that's the way it is now. *(beat)* And anyway, how can he be in charge when we don't understand each other? If I could speak their lingo it would be a start.

Louise   But we don't let them speak it. You even changed their names!!

Steve   Oh god, we had to, no one could pronounce them otherwise. They understood. It's for the good.

Louise   What do you mean?

Steve   Spent too much time with Daddy eh? Money kept ya nice and comfy. Ever get ya hands dirty? Work for a day? *(laughs)*

Louise   Yes, I have.

Steve   Yeah? Surprising. (*beat*) Look at the way they
                act, Louise. I mean, it doesn't bother me too
                much, makes me feel more stable. But you'd
                never see one of our families doing some-
                thing like that. Fighting in public!

Louise   No, we'd just stab each other in the back in
                private.

Steve   Oh, grow up, girl. Next you'll be giving me
                a lecture, 'be nice to the Maoris'. Look, I just
                say it how it is, how I see it. At least they
                know where I stand. I regret the way I said
                some things today, but I still stand by them.
                (*beat*) To you, I'm the bad guy, aren't I?

Louise   No.

Steve   Yes I am. But all I did is what I was told and
                became successful and that's what makes me
                the bad guy. Ya work hard, keep ya head
                down, and don't ask for nothing. Just like
                John, and look, he's getting ahead. (*beat*) I
                have as much right to this place as anyone
                else and you want to know why? Because I
                have the dead too. So don't you and your kind
                ever make judgement on me.

Louise   You don't trust anyone do you? Anyone. Me,
                because my family has money and John, be-
                cause he's a Māori.

Steve   I trust John, but I don't trust you. Not because of the money, no. I don't trust your kind and I know John and his family don't either. How far have ya gone? Eh? How far will ya go? Will ya be there for John and his family when the going gets really tough? Or will ya come in and out when it suits you? At least they know what I'm doing and that I'm doing good.

Louise   Listen to yourself. You say you're doing good. You treat them like only you can do them right. You do, I do, all of us. Sue was right. God, I didn't even hear her real name till today. *(beat)* We can't own them. My father tried to own me, so I left. Don't you see – you can't own people.

Steve   Okay, okay, so you got something there. But who's gonna take the first step? You? Me? Who's gonna take the punt? Go, 'here ya go mate, you have it, go for it'. Not me. I wanted to give John a go, I really did. But I can't, I just don't have it.

Louise   So what are you gonna say to them?

Steve   Nothing.

Louise   But they're expecting something.

BOYBOY *enters out of view.*

Steve   That's not my fault. I'm not gonna tell John he hasn't got the promotion because he's a Māori, not here anyway. The day's been a bloody shambles already. If he asks, I'll say the decision's out of my hands. I'll make something up to get us out of here.

Louise   You'll tell him later?

Steve   Not now.

LOUISE *notices* BOYBOY.

Louise   How long have you been there?!

Boyboy   I just got here. Everything's all ready, the cake and stuff. Mum got me to fetch you.

Steve   Well, hell, we can't keep your Mum waiting, or, for that matter your Dad, eh Boy?

Boyboy   No, we can't. I'll just shoot off!

BOYBOY *runs off. Lights fade on them and come up on the others.*

Amiria   Mum, Mum I need to talk to you. Why I got so drunk.

Sue/Wai   I know why, girl. You really hurt your father by doing that and now we have to work harder to make sure Mr Campbell has a good time. Forget about it girl, and give me a hand, that's the best way to let it pass.

Amiria	Mum, I need to talk to you.
Sue/Wai	Can it wait girl? We just want to finish the day good.
Amiria	I can't wait. Now. Please. Stop.

WAI *stops.*

Sue/Wai	OK girl, what do you want to tell me?
Amiria	I, I want to...
Sue/Wai	Spit it out. Hell, I don't have all day.
Amiria	Mum. Please!
Sue/Wai	(*noticing how tense* AMIRIA *is*) It's OK girl. I'm sorry. Way you go, eh?

HONE *enters.*

Amiria	Mum, I...
John/Hone	What the hell are you two doing? Yakking?
Amiria	Yeah, no... oh...
John/Hone	Where the hell's the present? They'll be back in a minute.

HONE *exits, tidying up.*

Sue/Wai   We'll fix it up later eh? Later, when we have a sit down.

WAI *exits*. AMIRIA *goes over to* RONGO. *She sits.*

Amiria   I'm leaving. I'm getting married. In Auckland, yeah Auckland. Moving up there with Nick, the Pākehā fella from the office. That's what I was trying to tell Mum. No one listens to me, talking all the time and no one listens.

Rongo   I am.

Amiria   I'm not hapū; it's love. We leave next week. Gonna be a real city girl, everything I ever wanted. I didn't get excited when he asked me. I just felt light, floating. My feet haven't touched the ground since. I wish they would. I'm gonna miss you Baby, I'm gonna miss you a lot.

RONGO *hugs her sister.* HONE *enters.* BOYBOY *comes running in.*

Boyboy   Dad! Dad!

John/Hone   Where are Steve and Lou?

Boyboy   On their way Dad. Dad!

John/Hone   Are youse right? (*to* RONGO) Come on Baby, cheer up eh. It really has been a cracker of a day, hasn't it? Full of surprises.

Rongo   Yeah Dad. Full of surprises.

Boyboy   Dad!

John/Hone Boy, what the hell do you want?!

Boyboy   He's not going to give it to you Dad! He isn't going to give you the job. The job Dad.

John/Hone Oh bullshit!

Boyboy   It's true. I heard them talking, down at the beach. He said he can't give it to you 'cause you're a Māori. *(beat)* What are you gonna do about it Dad?!

The TĪPUNA *call* RONGO *to join them. They are teasing her. She is pulling toward them. The others freeze. The call fades off. Normality returns.*

John/Hone Nothing. He's right. Ya can't, can you Boy? Ya can't have that.

WAI *enters with* RONGO's *present. She realises something has changed.*

Sue/Wai   John?

John/Hone There's no job, no promotion. No nothing. What a dreamer. *(to self)* Become a foreman, ha. Who the hell did I think I was?

Sue/Wai   What do you want to do?

John/Hone   I know what I'd like to do. *(beat)* He's still our guest and my boss. We do as we always do for guests. Treat them well.

Boyboy   But Dad, oh Jesus!

STEVE *and* LOUISE *enter.*

Steve   Oh, this looks superb Sue. So we're all set for the cake eh? That walk was great, made a bit of a gap. *(laughs)*

John/Hone   Beer?

Steve   Perfect.

John/Hone   Louise?

Louise   No thank you.

John/Hone   Boy.

BOYBOY *gets another flagon, fills up a glass for his father and then one for* STEVE. *He carefully gives one to his father.*

John/Hone   It was alright out there, eh?

Steve   Too right. Great guide in Lou. *(to* LOUISE*)* You should take up being a guide if you ever leave teaching. *(laughs)*

BOYBOY *then goes to* STEVE *with the other beer. He stands in front of him and then throws it over* STEVE's *face. There is general chaos.*

Boyboy   You're a bloody liar! You made a fool of my
                  Dad, eating our food and acting like a friend!

Steve   *(wiping his face)* What the hell?

Boy   I heard you, both of you down there. I heard
                  you, you bastard! Look at him. He knows! I
                  told him!

HONE *is silent.* AMIRIA *is enjoying it all. The* TĪPUNA *call*
RONGO *with the haka pōwhiri.* WAI *frantically tries to wipe
the beer from* STEVE. LOUISE *is stunned.* RONGO *is with-
drawing more and more. The* STRANGER *is at the front of the
group.*

Sue/Wai   *(wiping the beer from* STEVE*)* Oh sorry Mr
                  Campbell. I don't know what came over him.
                  (to BOYBOY*)* You stupid boy.

Steve   It's okay, it's okay.

Sue/Wai   *(to* STEVE*)* Let me take your shirt. John's got
                  a spare one in the car, haven't you John?

Steve   Stop it! At least you know what's going on.
                  I ah... my old man, he stopped it... no, I did.
                  I've got a bonus. *(he pulls it out)* That's the
                  surprise, John. You've still got a job, if you
                  were wondering. I just couldn't. Didn't have
                  the guts. No one would stand for it. No one.
                  I'm sorry mate.

Boyboy   Sorry! Sorry! Dad, aren't you gonna say any-
                  thing?! Do something! Do something!

John/Hone   Be quiet Boy. *(pause)* Stay. I want you to stay. I won't say please. But I want you to stay.

Boyboy   He was making fun of you!

John/Hone   Shut up Boy!

WAI *goes to speak.*

John/Hone   *(to* WAI*)* And don't you say a word either! *(to* STEVE*)* Stay, you are our guest. You never lied to me. You've always been honest like a blade. I was dreaming, thinking I could be foreman. Things haven't changed that much. Thanks for the bonus; it's appreciated.

There is a hesitation from STEVE. *He then nods.*

Steve   That's alright John, you deserve it.

John/Hone   I'll deal with the boy later.

LOUISE *steps forward.*

Louise   No, no you must forgive Boy.

John/Hone   Why?

Louise   Things have been hard for him lately. He was supposed to tell you himself, but it looks like it's up to me. *(beat)* He's been suspended from school. So forgive him. I'm sorry, Boy. I gave you a chance.

Boyboy   I didn't mean... I didn't mean to.

Sue/Wai   Louise.

Louise   It needed to be said.

Amiria   You stupid bitch.

John/Hone   You fucken little bastard! (HONE *strikes*
BOYBOY)
After bringing you up! You ungrateful bastard. That's what you are! Don't you see, we
work so hard and you throw it back in our
faces like it means nothing! Get away from
me! Get out of my sight!

*The TĪPUNA call RONGO. Distraught, she leaves with them.
The struggle with her leaving her family and going with the
TĪPUNA should be evident. No one notices her go. STEVE stops
HONE. BOYBOY gets up and attacks HONE, swinging and
punching at him.*

Boyboy   Come on then! Hit me! You bastard! Come
on! Come on! I'm not gonna take off like
Mahurangi. I'll fight ya. Go on!

HONE *explodes. He pushes STEVE off him to the ground. He
then starts toward BOYBOY, fist clenched.*

Boyboy   Go on, do it! Are you gonna hit me? Go on!
The only time you touch me is when you hit
me. *(beat)* All I ever wanted to do was please
you, but you wouldn't let me, would you? I

have your name, youse are the only Mum and Dad I know. I don't know no one else. (beat) She's right, I got suspended from school. I didn't get into a fight or nothing. It happened 'cause I fell asleep. All those days I got up early to help you deliver wood, Dad. I got so tired ya see, so tired. I fell asleep in class, that's all. One of the teachers grabbed me and dragged me out. 'You rude boy, how dare you!' He took me to his office and he caned me, I don't know how many times. After a few, he'd stand me up, have a look see if I was crying. I didn't Dad, I wasn't gonna cry. He kept hitting me, then after a while he stopped, knew I wasn't gonna cry. He made me stand up, 'I'll teach you' he said, and left the room. I felt sick, put my hand down to touch my leg. I couldn't feel nothing. Brought my hand back up, there was blood. He came back in the room with the headmaster. He said go to his office, that I was suspended. He said that striking a teacher was serious and I could've ended up in jail. But I wasn't weak Dad, I stood up to them. No, I'm not weak.

The TĪPUNA *pass across the stage challenging* HONE, *stating that they have his daughter. Still it is not picked up by the family. They exit. Everyone stands back from them.* BOYBOY *and* HONE *are not sure what to do. Long pause.* HONE *goes to* BOYBOY *and holds him.*

John/Hone   You weren't weak Boy.

Boyboy   Dad, I'm...

John/Hone   Just be quiet eh? *(beat)* It's been a long day, we should start packing up. *(to all)* Start getting ready for home eh?

He goes to STEVE.

John/Hone   Thank you for coming Steve, you're a good mate. *(he hands* STEVE *the bonus)*

Steve   You keep it, you deserve it. Sorry for stuffing up the day for you.

John/Hone   No you didn't, you brought good news. *(beat)* Lou, Louise thank you for looking after our son, we'll do that from now on.

Sue/Wai   Let's shake a leg eh? We'll get most of the stuff here. You men go sort out the hole and baskets and things. Rongo? *(looks around)* Girl, go and find Rongo, she should be here helping us. She'll be down at the beach.

AMIRIA *exits.*

Steve   What can I do?

Sue/Wai   Nothing.

Steve   What can I do?!

WAI *looks to* HONE.

John/Hone   You can come with me and fill in the hole, take the stuff back to the car.

They go to exit.

John/Hone   Boy.

He turns and exits with them. The women begin to clear up.

Louise   I didn't know that's what really happened with Boy.

Sue/Wai   Did you ask him?

Louise   No.

Sue/Wai   So you thought it was true?

Louise   No.

Sue/Wai   Well, why didn't you do something about it?

Louise   I don't know. When I heard it from the other teachers, it sounded true.

Sue/Wai   You know that boy, you should have asked him. He trusted you. You didn't look into it, and then blurted it out 'cause you felt guilty.

Louise   I suppose I did.

Sue/Wai   Yeah, you did.

The two women continue to clear the stage. LOUISE *begins to sing in an attempt to lighten the atmosphere. It is 'The Blue Beat'.* WAI *quietly joins in. A type of truce is achieved by the two. Once the stage is cleared,* HONE, STEVE *and* BOYBOY *enter.*

John/Hone   Jeez, it didn't take long for you to clear this up. *(beat)* Those two not back yet?

Boyboy   Do you want me to go and get them Dad?

Sue/Wai   No. Hone you go.

John/Hone   Eh?

Sue/Wai   You go, see what's taking them so long.

John/Hone   Alright.

He exits. WAI *begins to say a short karakia to herself.*

Sue/Wai   E aku tīpuna kua wehe ki te pō roa manaakitia ahau.

Louise   What's going on Sue?

Sue/Wai   Nothing, just to finish off the day.

Louise   Oh, it'll be alright. No fires, no flames, everything's calm now.

They all exit with the remaining gear, WAI *the last. The* TĪPUNA *enter. They bring in* RONGO. *It mirrors what happened earlier. They are singing a waiata tangi, 'Ko te Matarekereke'.*

Ko te matarekereke i ahau
I tōu wehenga, taukuri e...

Kāre a Aituā wāna titiro
ka kūtia rawatia ahakoa ko wai rā...

Takahia atu te ara e takahi-nuitia rā
e te tini, e te mano e...

Auē, taukuri e... kua wheturangihia koe...
E Rongo e... okioki, e moe[23]

AMIRIA *enters with them. She takes hold of* RONGO *and starts to drag her.*

Amiria   Hold on, hold on, I'll get you there. (*out*) Dad! Dad! Someone! (*to* RONGO) Sis, sis? You still here? Oh, oh, you're so heavy. Your hair, (*she brushes her hair aside*) sand in your hair. Baby, I'm sorry, I'm sorry for everything. If I say these things you'll come back, won't you? Baby, Baby (*out*) Dad! Help! (*to self*) So heavy, hold on... ah, ah, I'll get you there.

AMIRIA *takes* RONGO *to the middle of the stage.* HONE *runs on and discovers the two.*

John/Hone   What?... Bub, Jesus what happened?!

She doesn't answer.

John/Hone   Well, what happened?!

Amiria   (*in tears*) She walked into the sea. Something
              made her go into the sea.

John/Hone   (*pause*) Go and get your Mum, the others,
              everyone! Hurry!... go! Hurry up! Run!!

She exits.

John/Hone   Oh god. How did this... ?

He tries to revive her, bring life back into her body. Nothing works.

John/Hone   Breathe Baby! Breathe. Breathe! Why the hell
              don't you breathe?! Do it! Do it!

*The others arrive and enter. WAI stands away from everyone.
The TĪPUNA begin to stamp, staying constant throughout. They
are toying with the family. Everyone is trying to bring her back.
It looks as if it is futile.*

Boyboy   (*to HONE*) Mum! Mum!

Louise   We need to get her to a doctor!

Steve   John, we'll take her back in my car. It's faster.
              (*lifting her*) Come on, let's go!

Sue/Wai   No. Put her down.

Louise   Sue, we have to get her away.

Sue/Wai   Put her down.

106

Steve   John, Jesus!

Boyboy   Mum, what are you doing?!

Sue/Wai   Put her down!

Steve   John!?!

John/Hone   (sharp) Put her down.

STEVE *quietly puts her down.* AMIRIA *breaks it, realising what they have decided.*

Amiria   No! You can't give up! You can't!
BOYBOY *grabs her and tries to take her away.*

Amiria   Get away from me. Get away from me!

WAI *finally goes to* RONGO. *The others slightly part from her. She holds* RONGO *and begins to wail. The stamping continues and quietly builds. The wailing stops, and she then begins to say a karakia over the body.* HONE *joins her.*

Sue/Wai   Io matua kore. Kia tau te aroha ki tō
               mokopuna, āe.

John/Hone   Io matua kore, e aku tīpuna, mauria tō koutou
               mokopuna, tiakina ia, āe.

AMIRIA *breaks free. She attacks her parents.*

Amiria   What are you doing? Stop it! Stop it! Stupid
               Māori bullshit!

They take no notice of her. She grabs her mother.

Amiria   Stop it! Stop it! It's useless. What's it gonna
               do? Bring her back?!

HONE *goes to grab her. She pulls back.*

Amiria   (*to* HONE) It's your fault, you're the one who
               brought her here! She didn't want to come
               here. She's gone and all you do is throw empty
               words over her. That's all we ever do, empty
               words. She's gone, she's gone and it's your
               fault!

Sue/Wai   (to RONGO) I've got your present here Baby,
               your Nanny's comb. Now she'll be with you
               always.

*The stamping stops. Everyone is silent, except for WAI, who is
quietly wailing over the body. The TĪPUNA ready themselves to
take RONGO away, their task is all but done. HONE removes
himself from everyone else.*

John/Hone   I'm the one who brought you here.

HONE *turns away. He is alone. He strips his shirt from him to
be bare-chested and begins a haka of self-hate, self-loathing and
remorse.*

> *E i, taku mana ka riro*
> *Taku ihi ka kore*
> *Tēnei taku whakaparahako i ahau...*

Ngaukino nei, ko te aroha – tīhaehae ake
Taku matarehu e peneki ana te āhuatanga nei
nā...

Tukua au kia hinga... hei utu, hei utu
Tukua au kia taka... taku kairau hoki
Tukua au kia mate...
Tuohu ana te māhuna i taku whakamā
taku whakamā...
taku whakamā nei hoki e..
UPOKO-KŌHUA!... KŌURA MŌKAI HI!!!

The TĪPUNA *then strike up a karanga. This is to call* RONGO
to Hawaiiki. It is then as if HONE *has heard their call. He realises*
that her spirit is still with them. He has a chance to get her back.
His haka changes and he turns it at the TĪPUNA *for taking*
RONGO.

Kei mate au e... e kāo!
Kei mate au e... e kāo!

Nāku noa te kākano i rui, tēnaka,
māku tonu rā e pupuri e!!

Nāku noa te purapura nei... Tukua mai!
Ko ōna totorere... Nāku katoa!!
Ko ōna kōiwi e... Nō taku heke!!

He hekenga whakapapa rangatira e kore e wehe
i ahau...
Korekore rawa, korekore rawa e wehe,
e tuku e...
I... E!!

Realising what is happening, BOYBOY soon joins his haka. Some of it mirrors his father's. The two fight for RONGO.

> *Nāu rā pea ā hine... e kāo!*
> *Nāu rā pea ā hine... e kāo!*
> *Tēnā he toto rite, he kiritahi, he kōiwi pēneki*
> *i ōku nei*
> *Tirohia tōna pakari!!...Tukua mai!!*
> *Ōna i whakaaro ai!!... Nāku katoa!!*
> *Ko ōna tīpuna e!!... Nō taku heke!!*
>
> *Tēnā tū wairua mai e aku tīpuna kia kore ai ā*
> *Rongo e riro!*
> *Korekore rawa, korekore rawa, korekore rawa*
> *e wehe e tuku e...*
> *IE!!*

AMIRIA *is drawn to her father.* STEVE *and* LOUISE *stand beyond them all. This cacophony continues until the hakas finish. Near the end of both hakas,* RONGO *slowly stands and begins a short haka of her own. She has heard her family. She has come back. The family have beaten the* TĪPUNA. *The family freeze, looking down at where* RONGO's *body was.* RONGO *then begins to sing some of 'Tawhiti' as a farewell to the* TĪPUNA. *Its beauty should pierce the air. The* TĪPUNA *take over the waiata.* LOUISE *and* STEVE *remain back in disbelief.*

The TĪPUNA *leave.* HONE *says a short karakia to close the door behind them. All call 'Tihei Mauri Ora!' to begin again. The lights fade.*

End.

Translations

Page 15

Alas...	*I cry for you my place of origin now left saturated in my tears*
Alas...	*the place where my umbilical cord is still attached and pulls at my heart with almighty strength*
Ranginui...	*Bear witness upon me as I leave behind all I know, all I am, including...*
Papa...	*Land walked upon by generations many before me As I now wander (seemingly) aimlessly in search of well being.*

Page 16

Leader	*The move is on!* *The move is on!*
Chorus	*Now we leave, just a few to a horizon far from sight to find physical sustenance...*
Leader	*Oh the bright lights!*
Chorus	*Flicker like stars!*

Leader   *People, so many people!*

Chorus   *White-skinned people! Show me what you have*
to benefit me, and all your challenges also...
that I may experience the sour and the sweet
and all that awaits me in the new, fast-changing
world!

Page 29

Far away is Hawaiiki, so distant
And Rangiātea in all its splendour
Alas, so far away...

Oh, so warm is my beautiful land
Across the great ocean of Kiwa
Alas, so far away

Let your wairua fly to the origin of our customs
and ways to the seed bed of words
Sown of Rangiātea

How lonely my heart aches for those ways of old
and the source of revitalising energy
the being I once was, now buried inside me

I long to climb the Aka Matua as did Tāwhaki
But let not your hands touch the Aka Taepa

My worth, my prestige is gifted to me by my
tīpuna

My strength cannot be found in this loneliness
But in great numbers, with my people

Far away.... so far away.

Page 31

Here, we welcome you
As I call my descendants to gather together sweet
child…
Enter, enter
Te korokoro-ā-te-Parata sweet child...

Listen carefully as my beckoning call is all
alluring
Like stars in the night

All my power, and awe, and energy
Drawing you closer - you are powerless to stop it...

Come closer, come closer, come with us!!

Pages 42-43

Leader   Burn... fire... burn...

Chorus   I search, and I search, for the driving force of
the human spirit.
Allow your thoughts to be known, set them free
That the truth be known!!

Leader	*It gnaws at my very soul!!*
Chorus	*And drives me insane!!*
Leader	*It bites at my flesh!!*
Chorus	*It stops me distinguishing between right and wrong!!*
Leader	*It eats inside me... !!*
Chorus	*There, such is the cost of holding deep within the secrets we keep, the price is a heart torn to pieces!!* *AUĒ HI!!*

Page 104

I am numb all over
Now you have left me, alone... why?!

Death itself is indiscriminate
Death comes in its own time to all of us...
no matter who

Now, your journey sealed, you walk a path
A path travelled by those who lived, and died,
so you could be

Alas, my child... you have become
one of the night stars
Oh Rongo... rest now, sleep

Afterword

Waiora is set in 1965 and returns to a time when many Māori families, and especially Māori youth, left the lifestyles of the past and moved to cities. Thereupon, as the first production's director observes in his programme note, "[s]tatistics illustrate the pain which followed". Partly this play exists to create a sense of that pain for readers and audiences today, Māori and Pākehā alike. Partly it urges us to ask ourselves what can be done about it, now. But, I venture to suggest, this sense of historicity also encourages a closer examination of racial identity for what it was, is, or might be.

The play opens upon a hāngi at a beach somewhere outside Christchurch. It is eighteen-year-old Rongo's birthday and her immediate family are there to celebrate, but they also register their sense of isolation from relatives 'up north'. The family, recently arrived in the city from their homeland, have lost whānau by moving south but also, it is shamefully and painfully disclosed, they have lost another son and brother with the noble name of Mahurangi, who may be alive or dead. The sense of loss is centrally emblematised by Rongo's mourning for her grandmother and her lack of songfulness: it is a spiritual loss. Her name is both ironic and prophetic: 'peace', and also 'to listen/hear/obey'. It also means 'news' - but what news?

Historically, Māori may really have been, in 1965, near to losing their language, and a major strand of the play enacts the significance of this by allowing important sections of the performance to stand untranslated. Boyboy is strapped at school for speaking Māori; Rongo's sister Amiria prefers the Beatles to waiata Māori; and their father probably never knew the words of songs he says he has forgotten. In the cast list he is identified as John/Hone but he's always called John in the play, and the same loss is pointedly remarked on for his wife Sue/Wai Te Atatu.

Their hāngi takes hours of preparation and draws on traditional tasks and gender roles. They have invited two guests, manuhiri to themselves as tangata whenua, and, even as the story cringes through its domestic embarrassments, the dignity of the hosts/natives-of-the-place towards their guests remains clear and moving. There seem to be no English words to translate the meaning of 'tangata whenua' at a hāngi at a beach away from home, and this in itself might indicate the loss and the confusion that Kouka begins to explore.

The play is structured on Aristotle's and Ibsen's dramatic formula of presenting only the as-it-were final 'fifth act' as the outcome of earlier events, often precipitated - as here - by the arrival of a stranger. The device economically and theatrically allows a domestic tragedy to reverberate with larger dimensions. John/Hone can't be made foreman because he's Māori, and we discover it's his own violence that has driven his older son away. Boyboy is in trouble for falling asleep in class and then beaten further for not crying; Amiria copes with it all by getting drunk; their mother Sue is defensively conservative; and Rongo does not hear what she knows nor know what she hears.

The arrival of the guests instigates the mounting climax of the play. One of them, Steve, is the original mill-owner's son, gawky and well-meaning, and the other the schoolteacher Louise Stones. Steve, John/Hone's boss, and much younger

than John/Hone, says: "Me, I was born here; it's home, part
of me ... It's the land, ya understand that ... the bond with the
land. It's home when ya work the land."

It is such a simple statement, full of both warmth and inno-
cence, and a horrible ignorance. It's a daring move by the
playwright and a thunderous moment theatrically - yet made
so simply. The complexity of responses which readers and
theatre-goers might make to this moment could serve to sum
up all of colonial history in miniature, and no less clearly for
that, yet not in black-and-white either.

At the play's first production at Downstage, a beautiful and
luminously mirroring set of sea and sky was used to evoke
the beach and to suggest various other kinds of marginality
"adrift from any recognisable cultural setting". In his programme note the designer went on to say that "the parting of
mirrors has loose references to Rangi and Papatuanuku and
the creation of the world". The Māori creation myth, perhaps
unlike the Christian one, enacts not only a sense of the struggle of existence but also the violence and cost of asserting any
selfhood, personally or for a would-be sovereign nation.

So at this hāngi at this point in time, the forces, tides, weeds
and wrack of a colonising past swirl around one family and
one daughter, and almost sweep her, and them, away. Other
nations and languages have indeed disappeared in the history
of humankind and this - almost - is another. Rongo says, 'I
left because I thought we had lost those words, those sounds'.
But though called to Hawaiiki by the tīpuna, she will not,
and she cannot, go there. The struggle of Rongo at the end
is not between coloniser and colonised; rather it is a struggle,
to and fro, between the forces of life and death as they exist

and continue to exist in a post-colonial nation, performed here on the floor of a (post-) colonial theatre.

The tīpuna emblematise this struggle in the sound of the karanga calling Rongo away. Her father hears this and turns his waiata of grief and remorse into a haka of defiance. Boyboy and Amiria join in with him to create a range of voices and emotions which in performance is gripping and terrible. In this way, Rongo's spirit is saved from self-drowning.

* * * * * * * * * * * * * * * * * * * *

I am aware that what I say here as a Pākehā may be inappropriate, misguided or at best peripheral - the skewed stance that denies otherness. One could certainly argue that this play gives an astute sense of the roles and constructions of gender as they prevailed thirty years ago, roles which may or may not have changed much. But what of the roles of racial identity? Could it be true, paralleling Simone de Beauvoir's analysis of being a woman, that one is not born but rather becomes Māori, or Pākehā? Is it the case that one's sense of identity is coterminous with one's physical characteristics, or is race also, like our present understanding of gender, in some way 'constructed'?

All stage performance, of course, has people acting in roles that are 'put on', not excluding the ethnicity and gender of their enacted characters. With ordinary realism which aims to replicate everyday life on the stage, where the staged event seems close to everyday life, audiences may not notice this. But theatre can also serve to remind us that everyone 'performs' in how they dress and present themselves, how we display our sense of gender, class or lifestyle. It's a powerful effect in the theatre when a performance consciously foregrounds sexuality or gender as roles (by cross-casting, or by other modes of theatrical non-realism). In this way we may come to perceive aspects of our everyday social life as not innate but 'acculturated' - produced by the culture or cultures around us. To suggest that racial identity too is something learnt, and like other roles of identity can change over time and within individual or group experience, may seem less acceptable. But racial identity enacted as such on the stage presents us with a new environment in which to consider racism.

A marginalised group - here, Māori - seeking to redress its marginalisation in relation to another culture, has a potential for intervention in three (not necessarily sequential) phases. The first is the demand for equality, for a fair share in the status quo. Not long ago Māori actors and theatre-goers wanted more and better representations of Māori on the stage. Then, partly from frustration at the failure of the first phase, a second stance emerges, when people want to reverse the values of the status quo. This stage tends to be separatist, culturally rich, sometimes aggressive. Māori theatre companies and Māori-language productions perhaps exemplify this stance. The second stage is necessary to create a sense of community and keep up energy, but it provokes anxiety since it creates a new set of boundaries to be policed. And it's vulnerable to a re-reversal: to backlash. It may be dangerous because it continues to enshrine the rigid differentiations of binary thinking and the oppression that results from that.

There is however a third possible stance, which is to question, destabilise or undermine the whole structure of current thinking with its concepts of dominance, rather than simply reversing them. This sort of analysis may not seem a politically useful tool for anti-racism work, because it's reflective and analytical rather than pro-active. But without scrutinising the notion of binary oppositions and with them our present concepts of racial identity, the structures of oppression will never change.[1]

This kind of self-reflective analysis is something that theatre is good at. Of all the arts, live theatre can best engage with difficult questions since theatre plays with possibilities - beginning with the possibility of 'acting out' another person's personhood. Kouka's *Waiora* is a sombre work but it is beautifully and play-fully exploratory.

It's notable that this new play, like Kouka's other most recent one, the acclaimed *Nga Tangata Toa: The Warrior People*, is set back in a historical time used to reflect on the present. *Nga Tangata Toa* is based on Ibsen's early Norwegian nationalist saga *The Vikings at Helgeland* and transposes a mythic story from another country's past onto the colonial history of Aotearoa New Zealand. In making such a 'translation' Kouka had to consciously decide which historical moment from our own history to choose. In the event the story was set at the end of the First World War but other periods were (I believe) considered - World War II? The Korean War? By asking audiences to think historically and to look at people's sense of racial identity nearly eighty years ago, a sense of distance and comparison is created that renders both the past and the present relative to each other.

In style *Waiora* may seem almost televisual, working on a smaller scale than *Nga Tangata Toa* with familiar characters and a domestic story-line, in comparison with the other's dramatic Romanticism. *Waiora* is also, however, both realist and more than realist, in the poetic aspects of some of its writing and especially in the theatrically stunning use of the chorus of tīpuna, who appears as both physical and real, and hauntingly abstract. It is the chorus of tīpuna who give this play its dimensions of loss and dream - the dream of loss, the loss of dreams - and, in the performance of haka especially, its spine-chilling abrasiveness and complex sense of resistance.

Perhaps because it is so emotionally and culturally rich, the imagery of *Waiora* may not always be fully accessible to a Pākehā audience. I think the play serves not to mourn a passing, nor to declare resistance, but to interrogate the nature of that which may - perhaps - be dying, and to gesture towards a range of possibilities for life. The audience is given a sense of this complexity most notably in the ambiguities of the play's ending. Rongo's death-wish - if only penultimately - is to be drawn on or back to Hawaiki. *Waiora* thus might itself be a waiata tangi, or it might not. Such a script is a moving showcase for Māori writing and dramaturgy, as well as for the performance arts of speech, waiata and haka. More than that, it offers to all who, like Rongo, can listen, a theatrical sense of wairua and a spirited, spiritual dramatic experience.

Judith Dale

[1] For a convenient summary of these three phases of intervention in feminist terms, leading to the post-structural or deconstructive analysis outlined here, see Toril Moi, *Sexual/Textual Politics* (Methuen 1985), pp 12-13.

122

He tohu aroha tēnei   A gift of love
Nā te whānau ō *Waiora*   from the cast and crew of *Waiora*
Te Ūkaipō   *The Homeland*